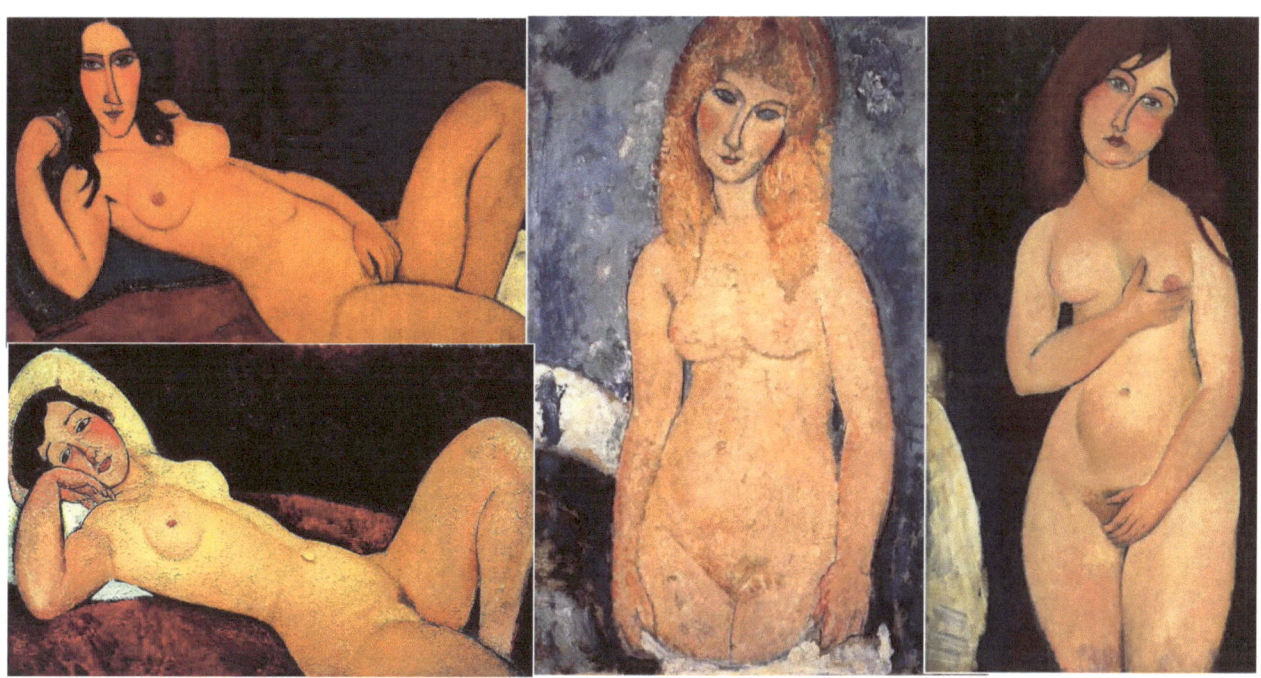

Amedeo Modigliani

Edited by Lacey Belinda Smith

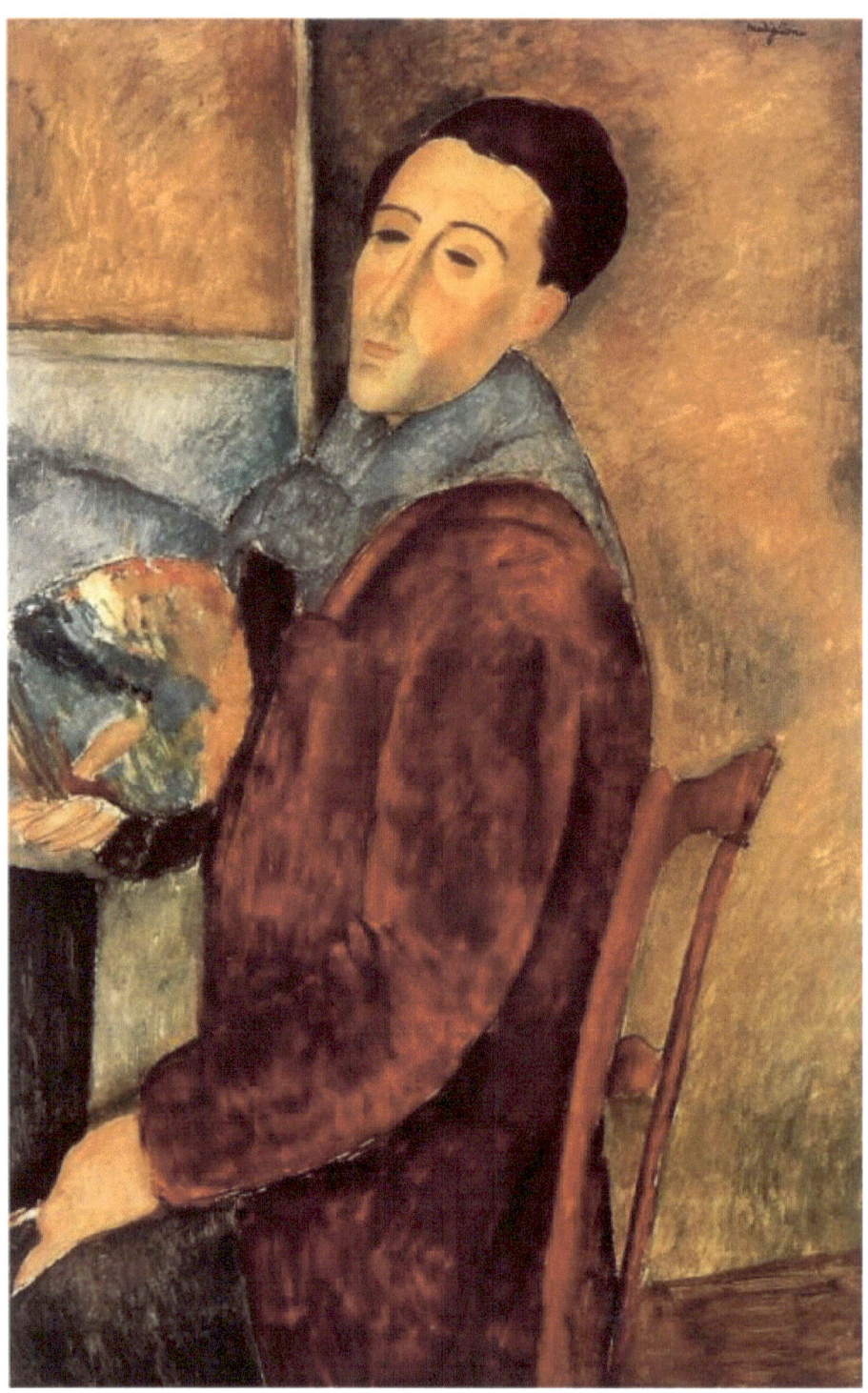

Self Portrait--1919
Amedeo Clemente Modigliani (1884 – 1920) was an Italian painter and sculptor.

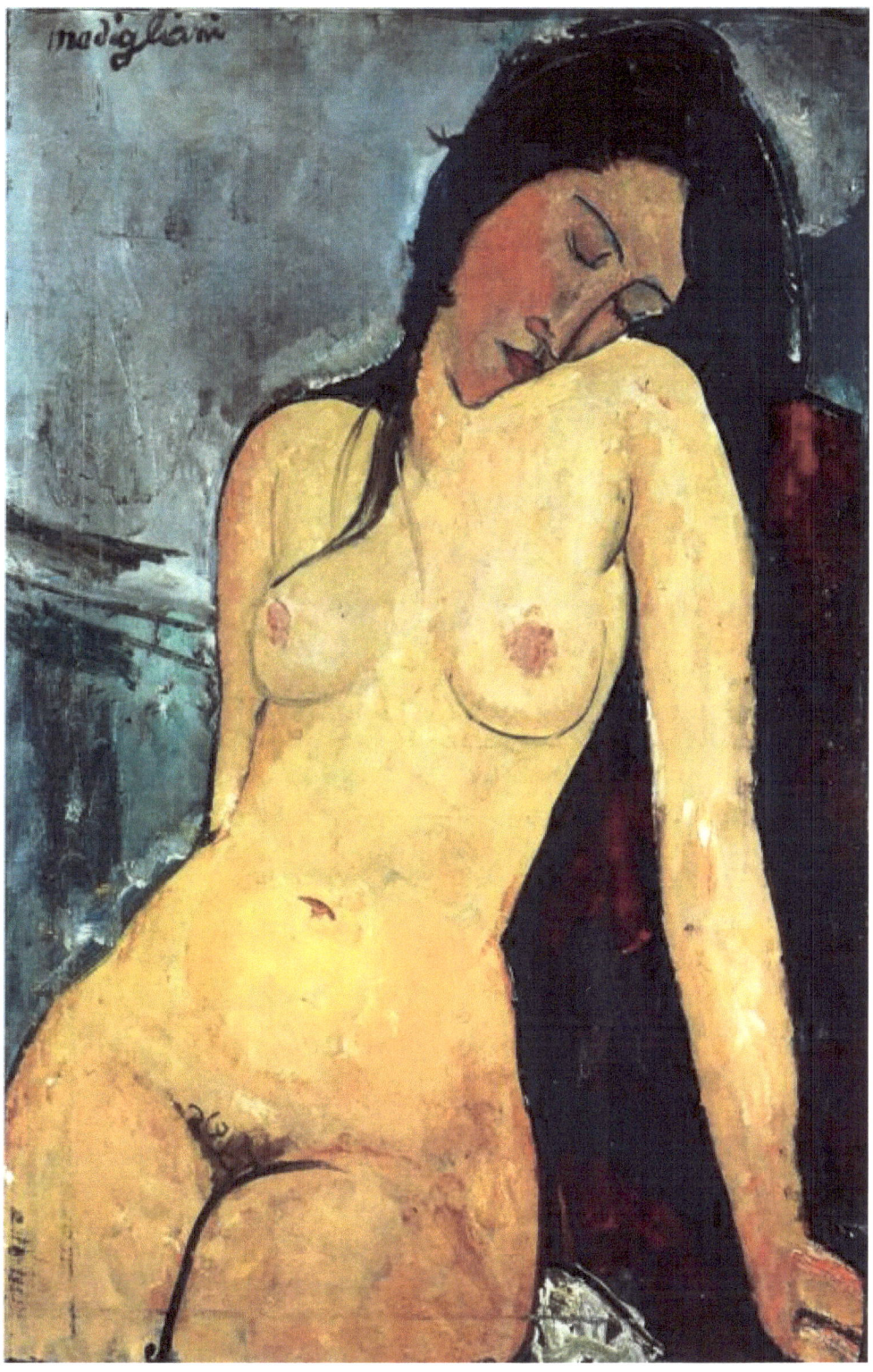

Seated female nude--Amedeo Modigliani—1916--Expressionism

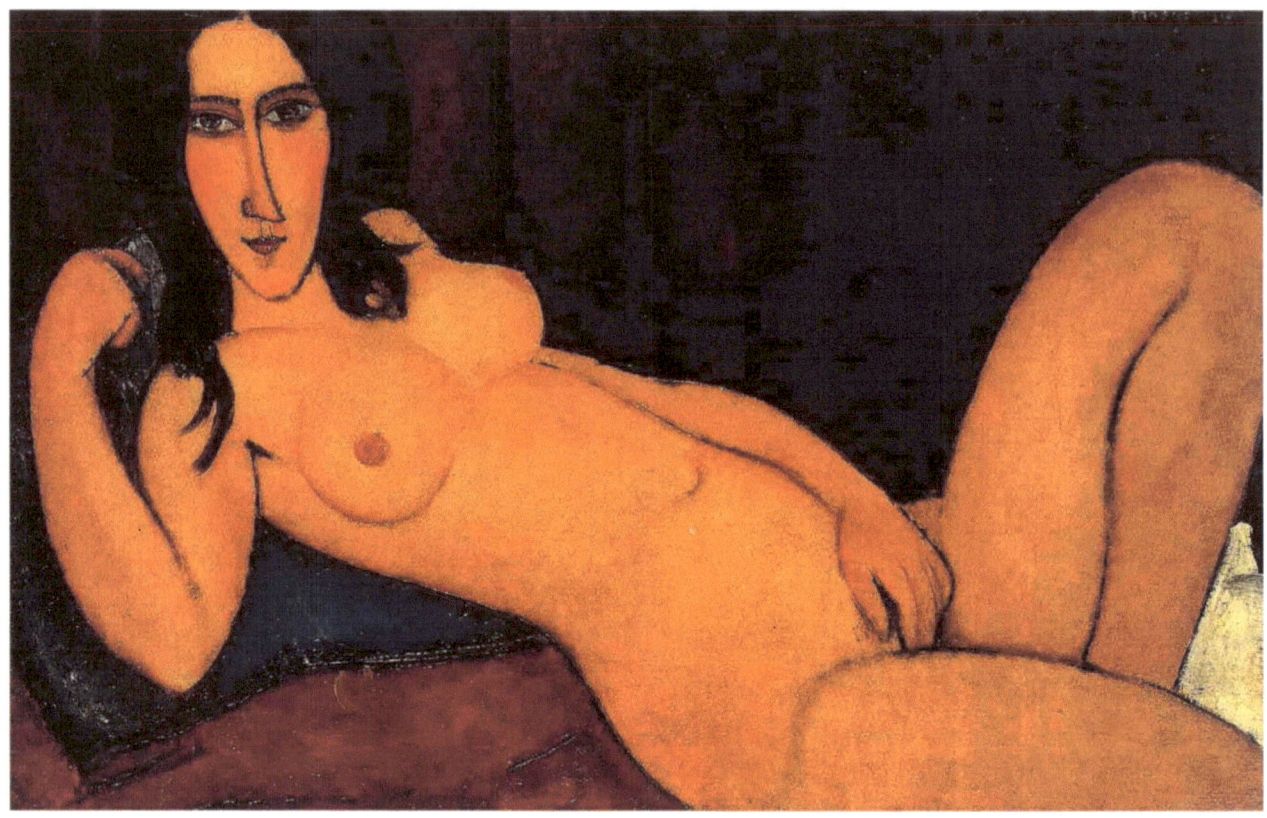

Reclining nude--Amedeo Modigliani—1917--Expressionism

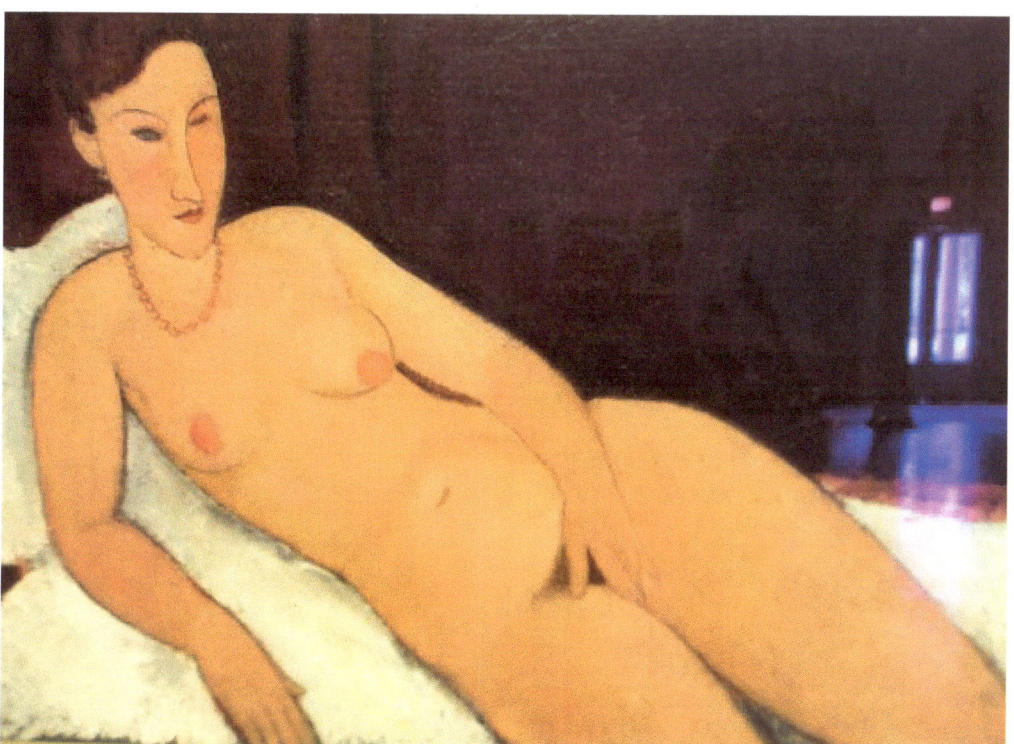

Nude with Coral Necklace—1917--Expressionism

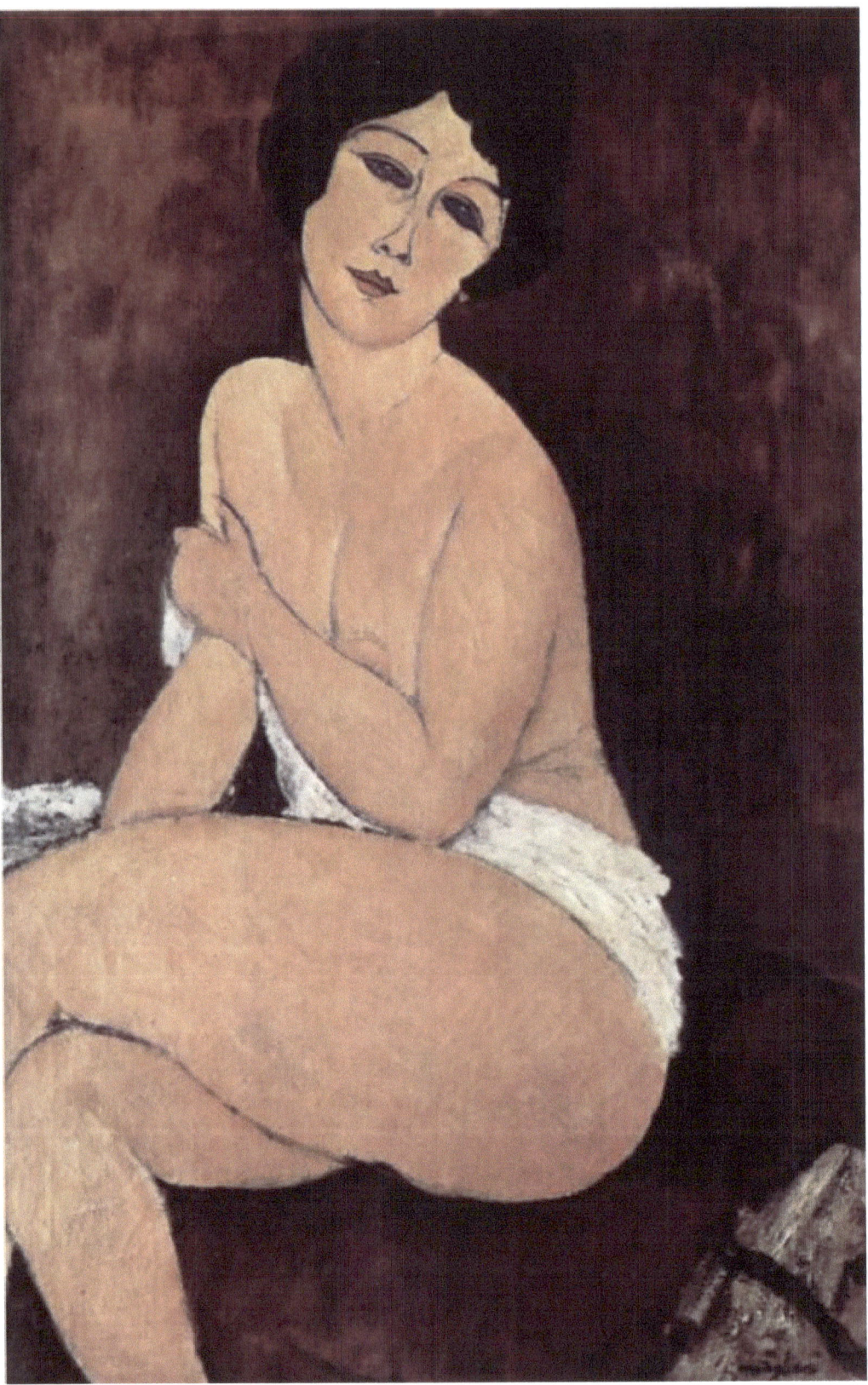

Nude seating on a sofa—1917--Expressionism

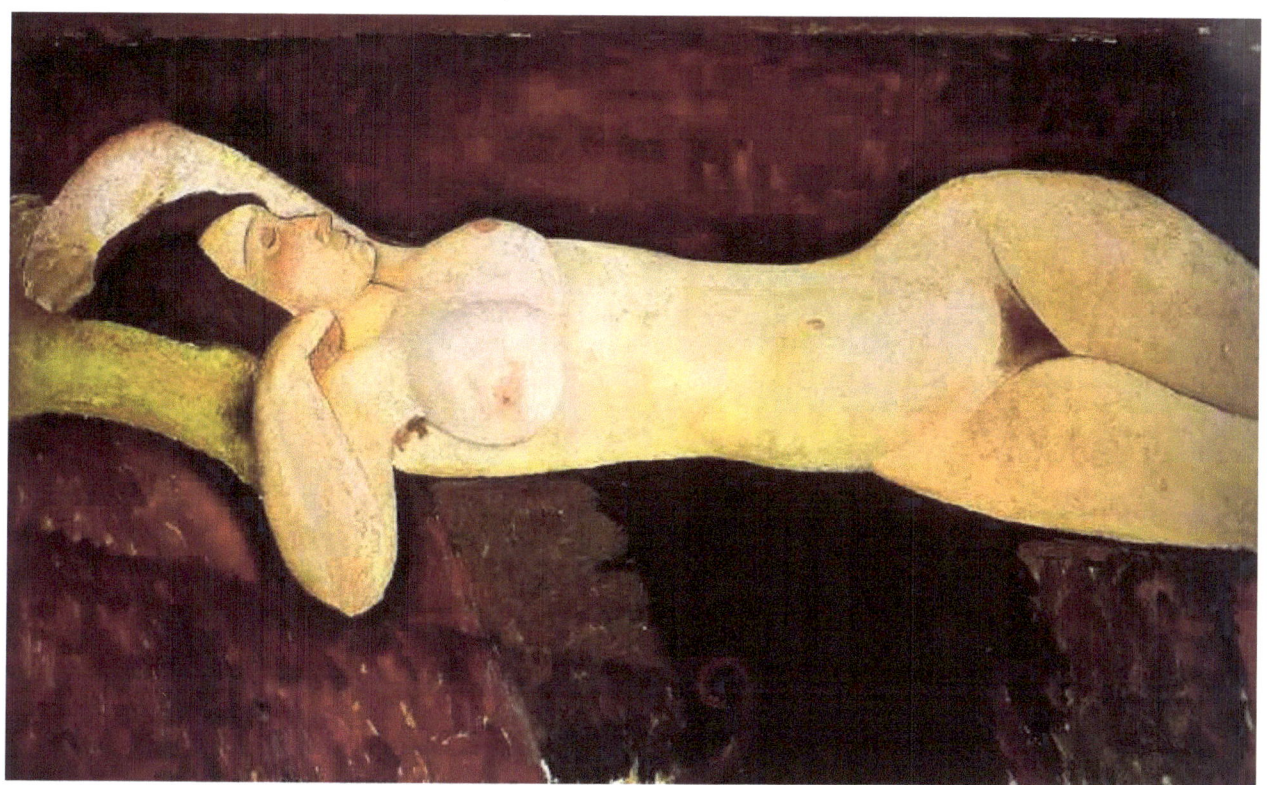

Le grand Nu (The great nude)—1917

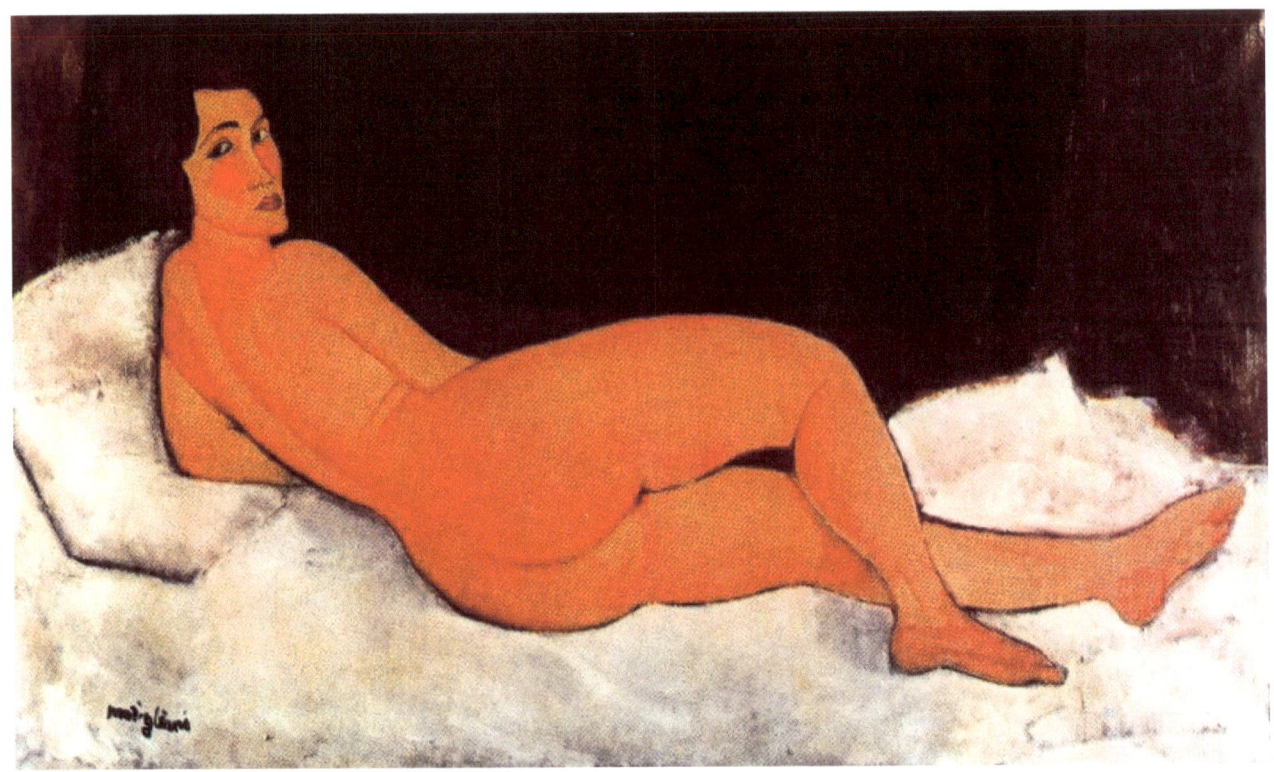

Lying nude-- 1917

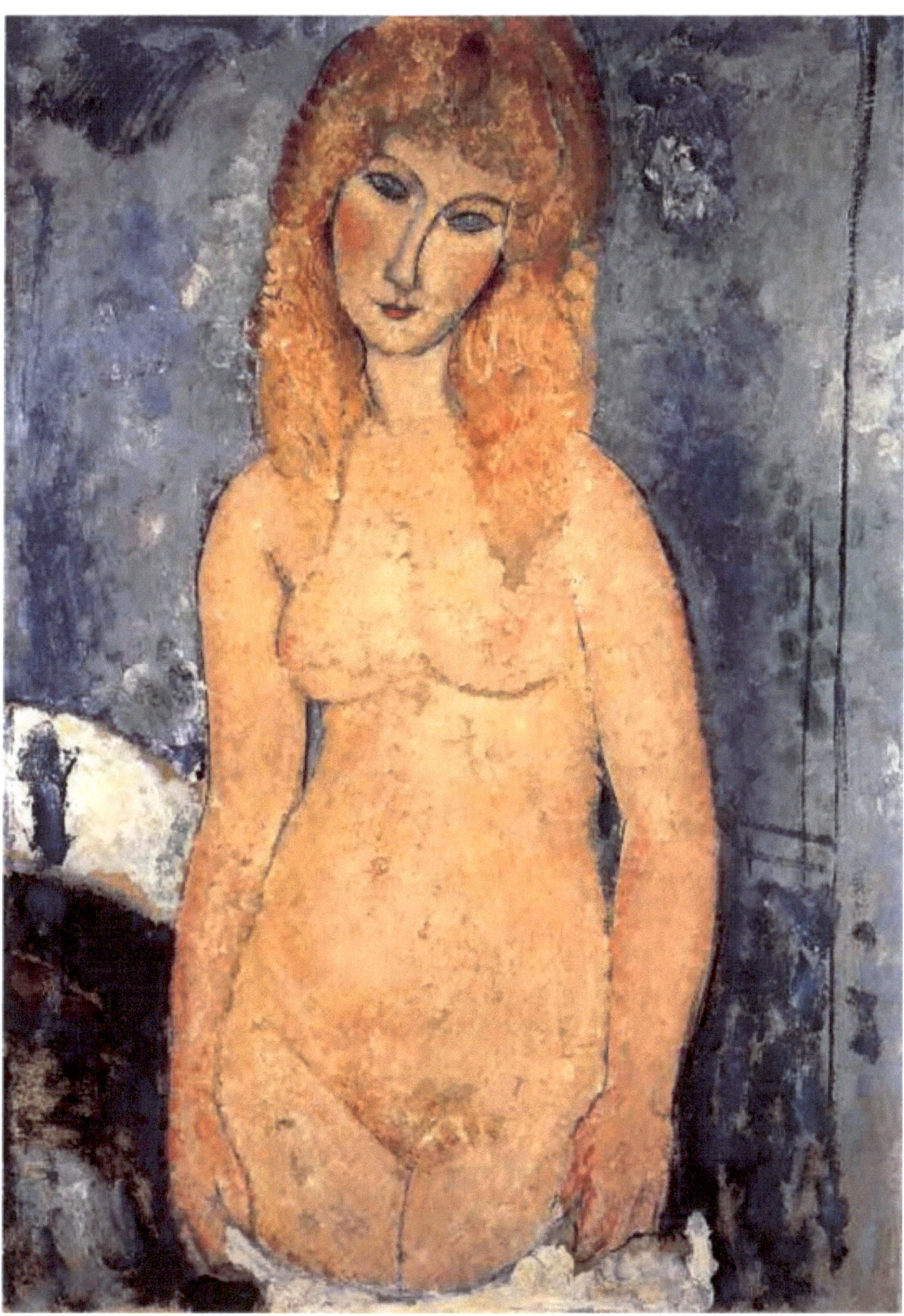

Blonde nude--1917

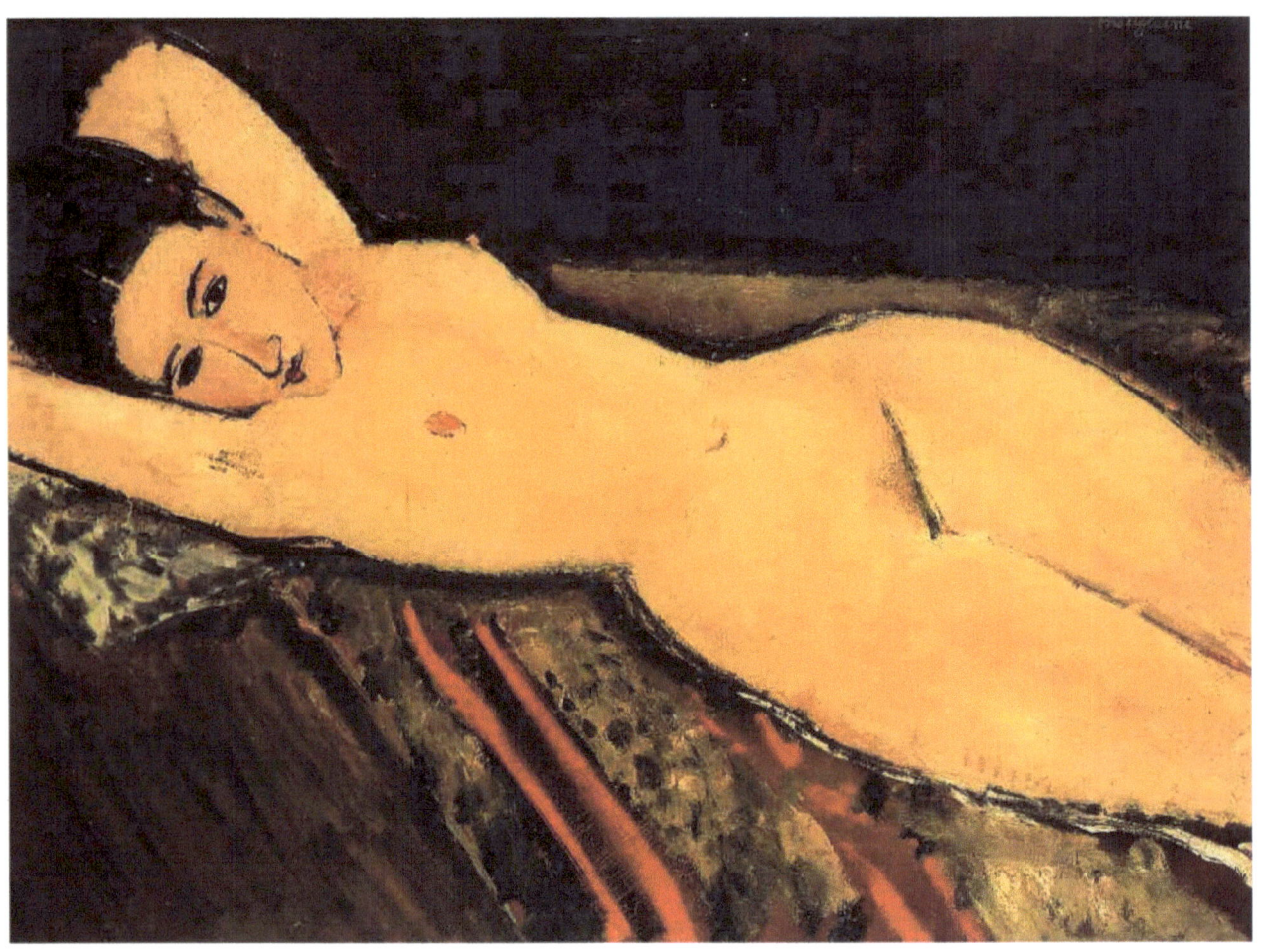

Reclining nude with Arms Folded under Her Head--1916

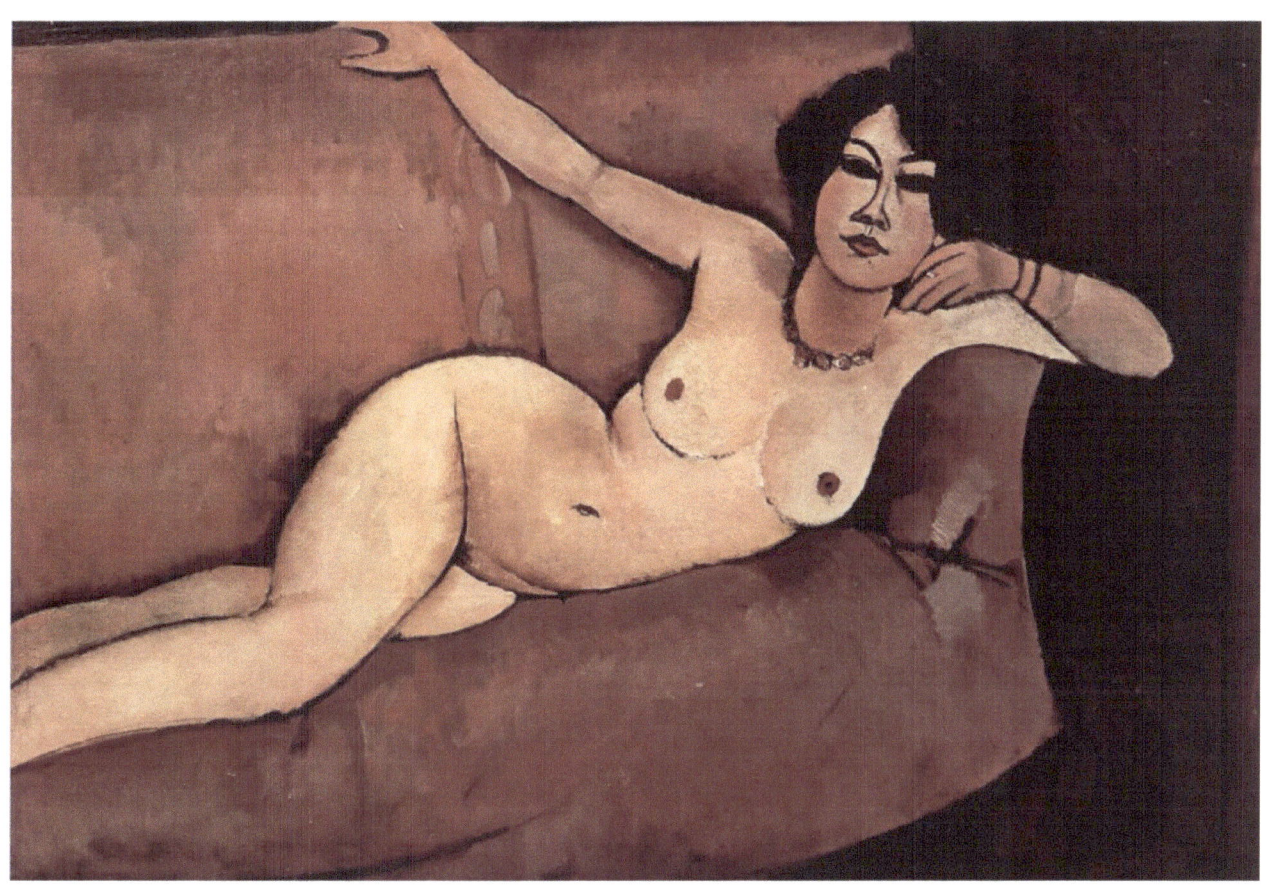

Nude on sofa (Almaisa)--1916

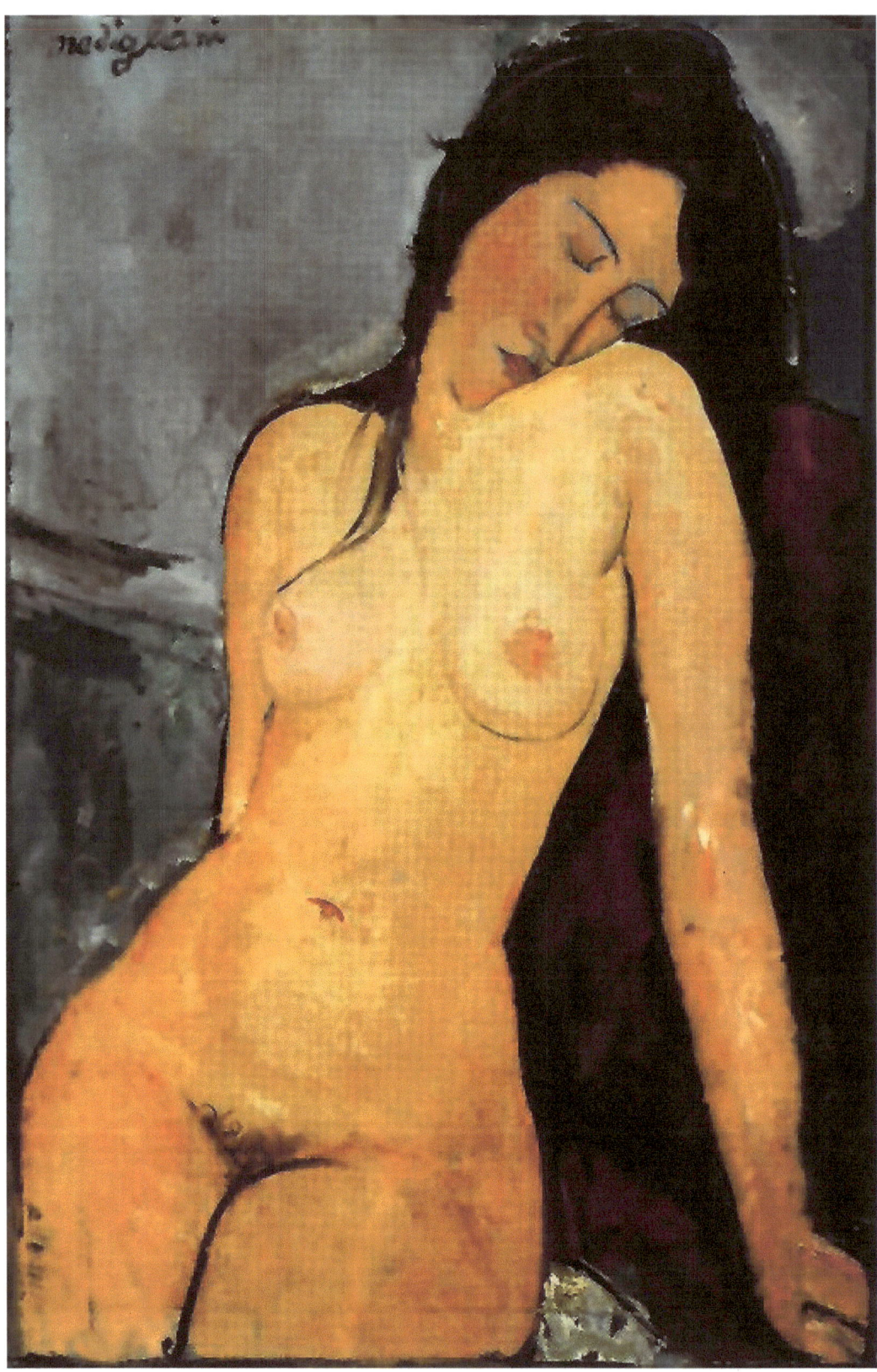

Female nude--1916

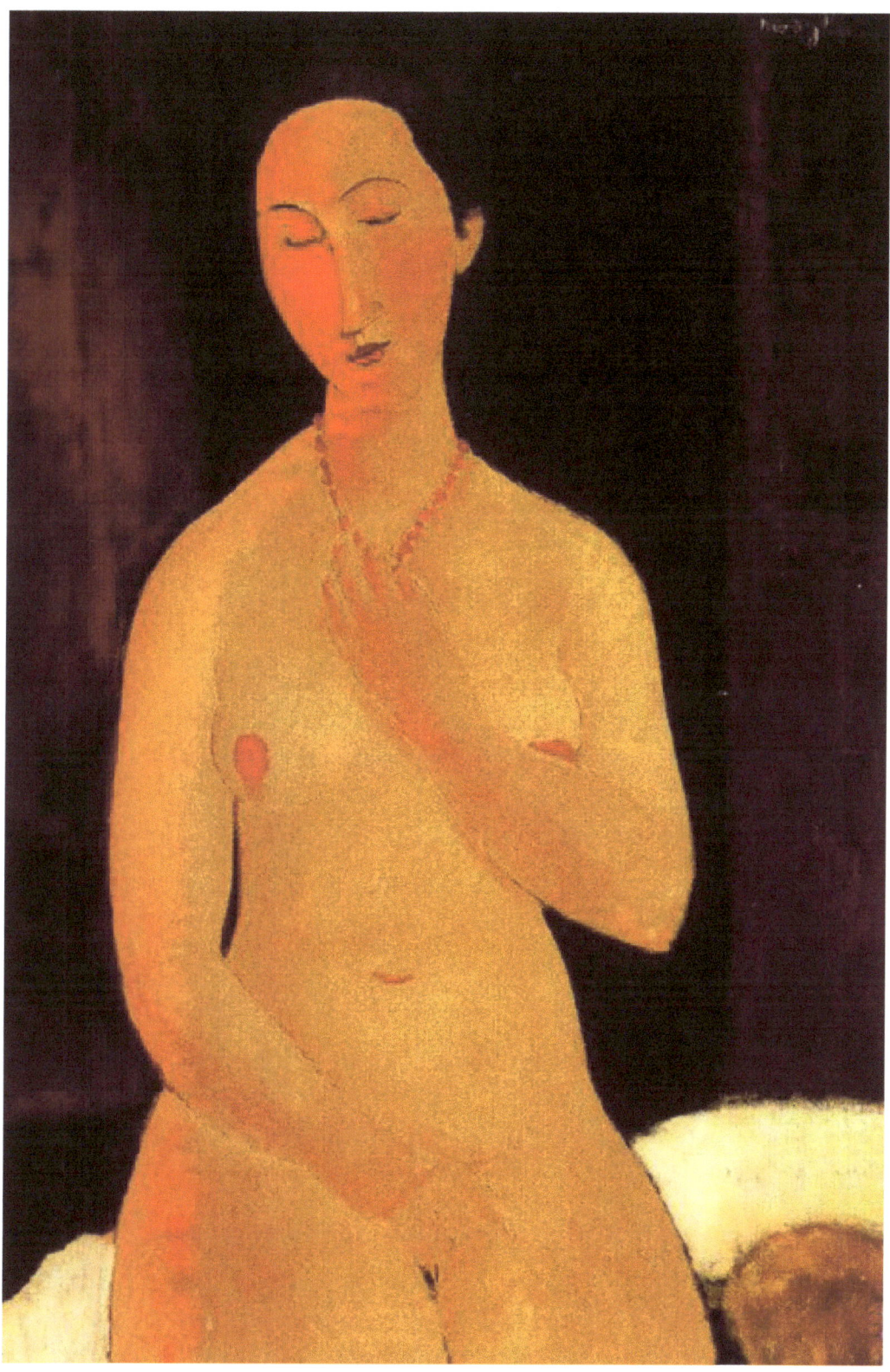

Seated nude with Necklace--1917

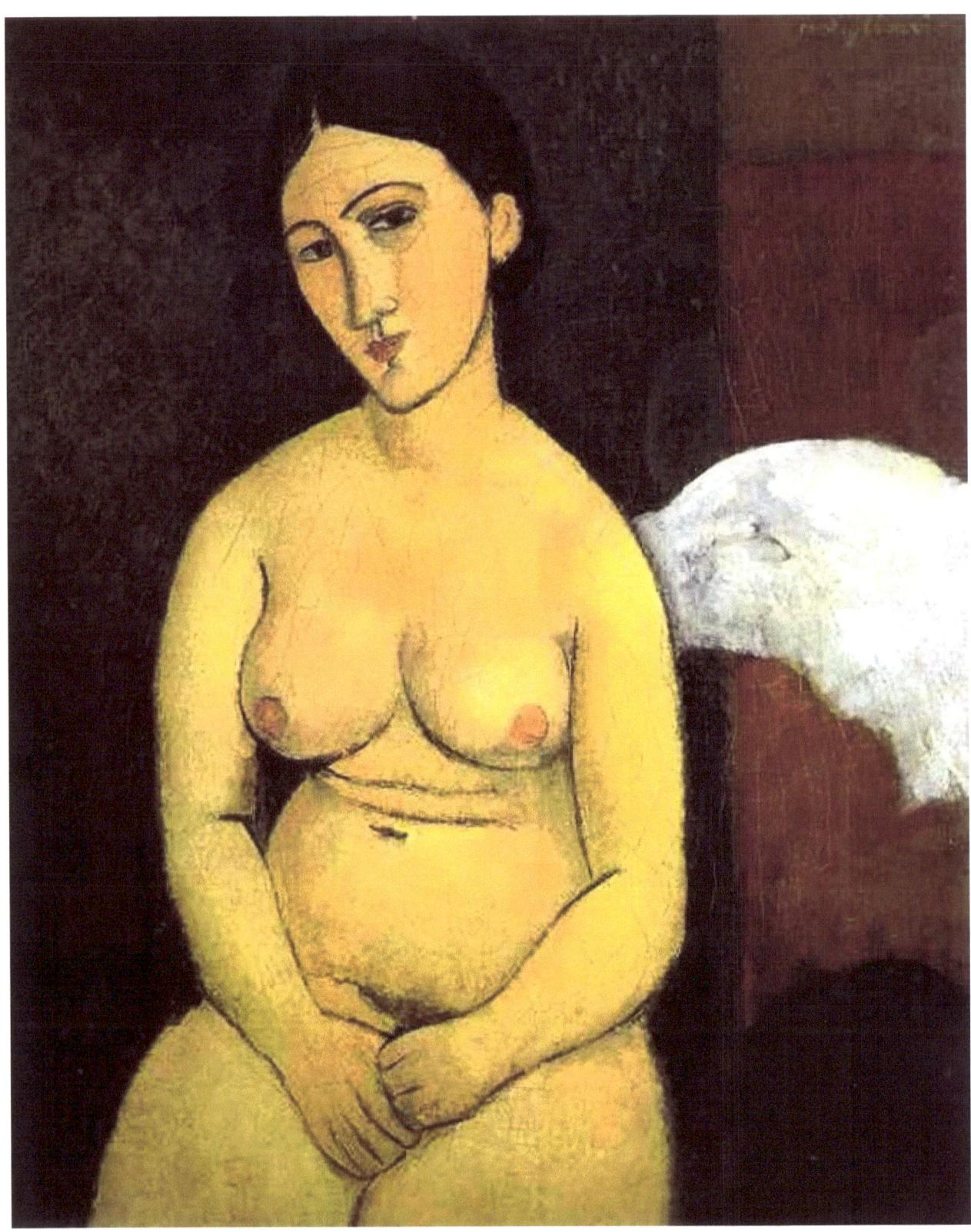

Seated nude--1917

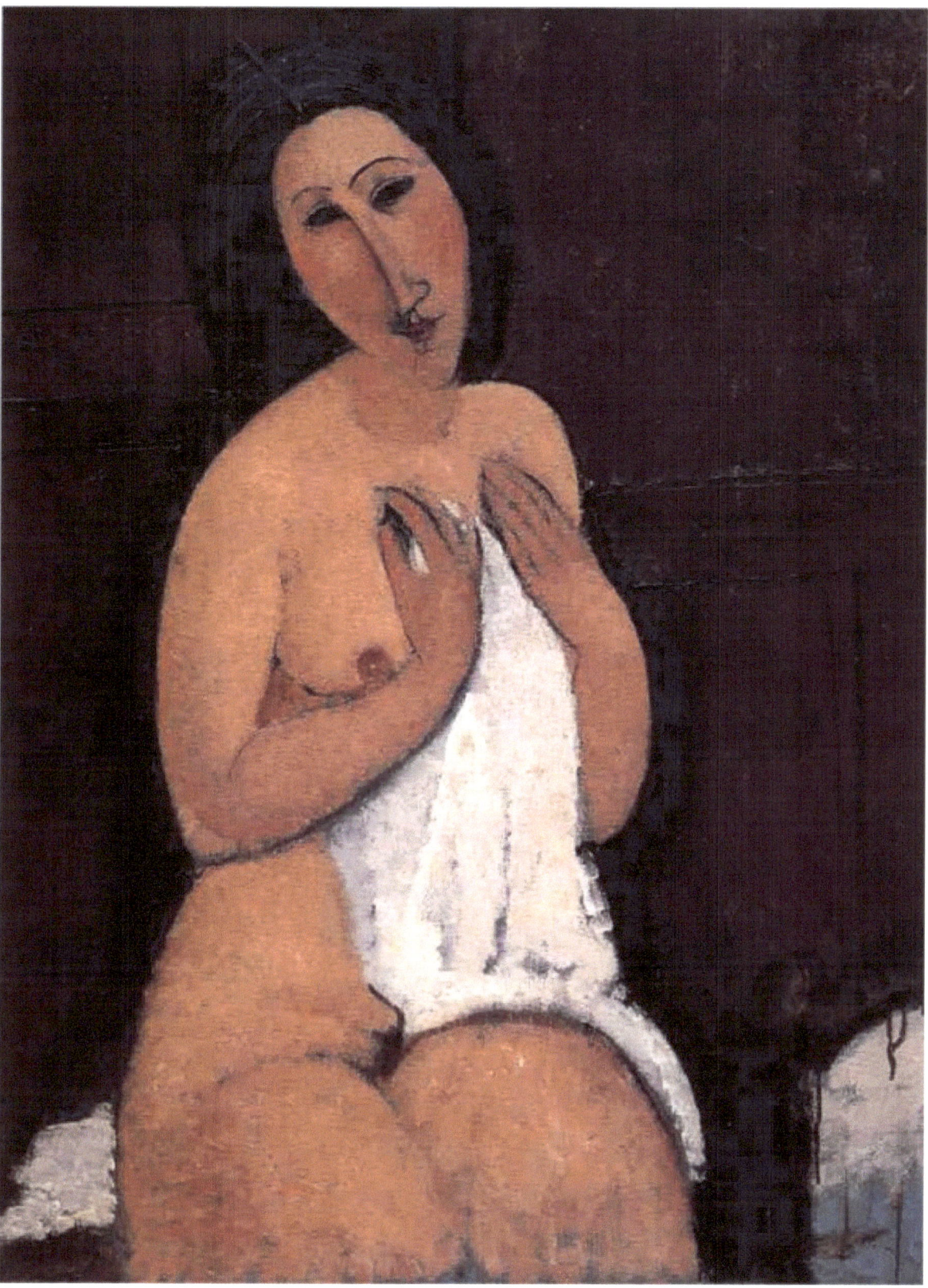

Seated nude with a Shirt--1917

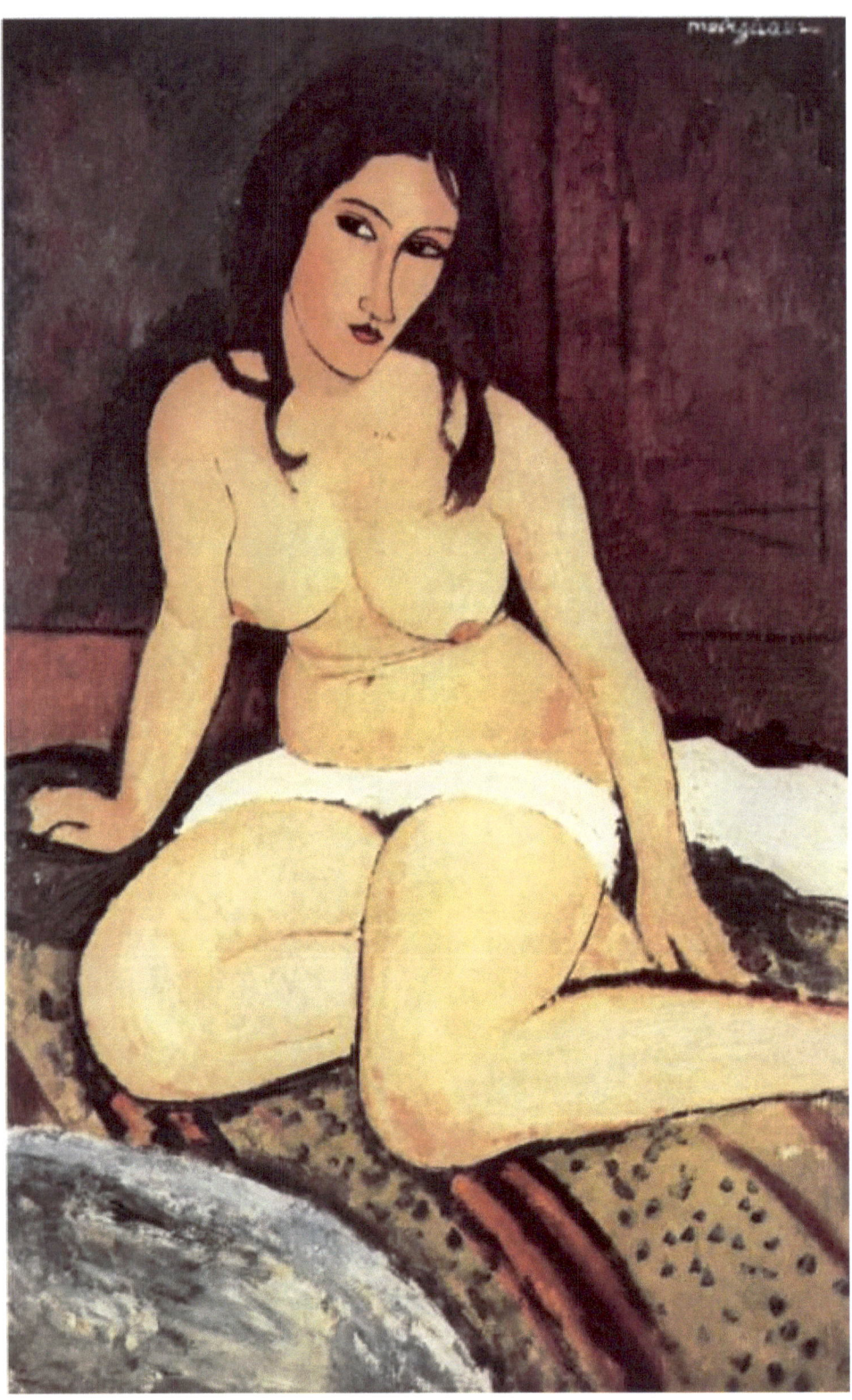

Seated Nude-- 1917

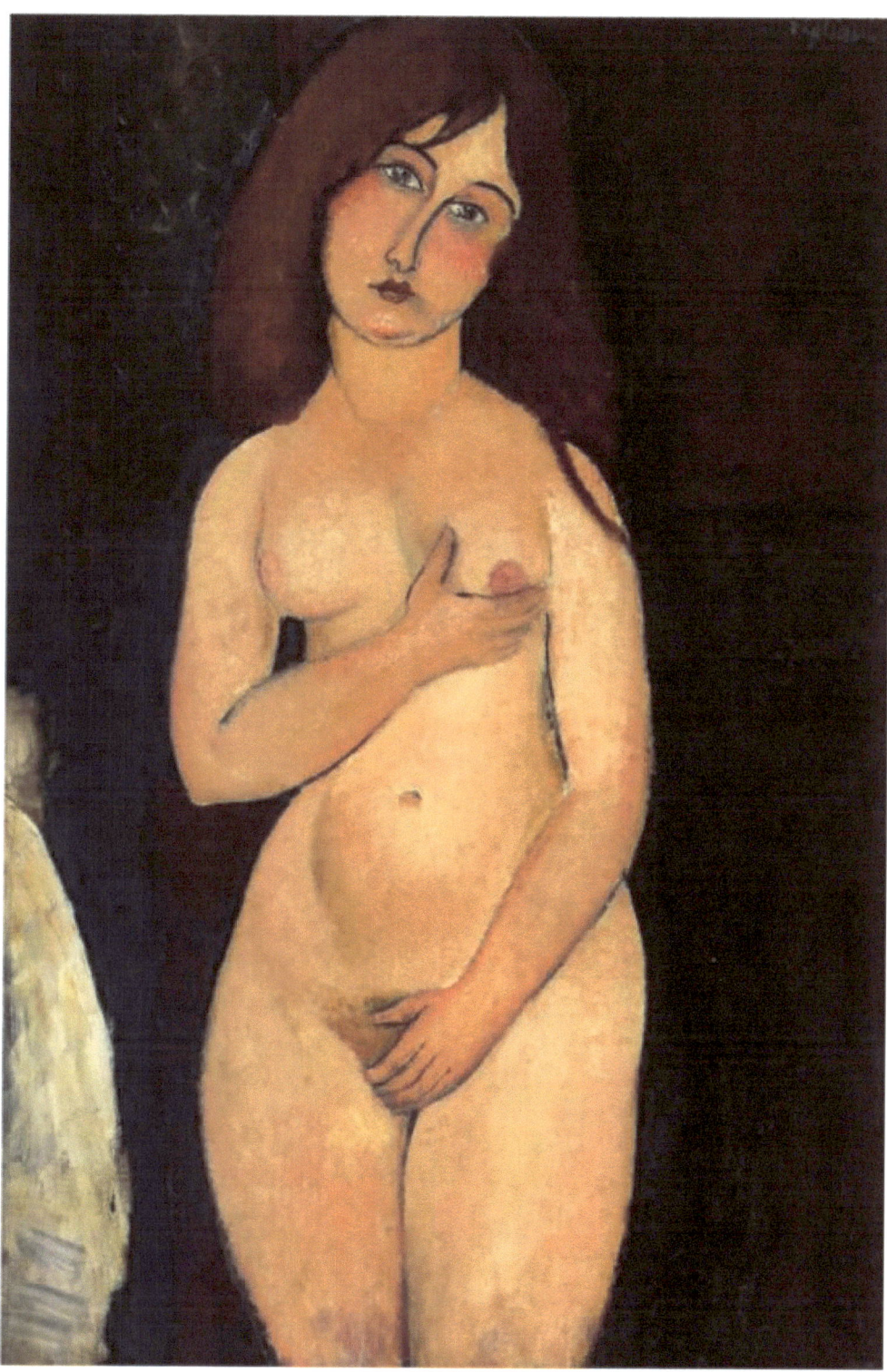

Venus (Standing nude)--1917

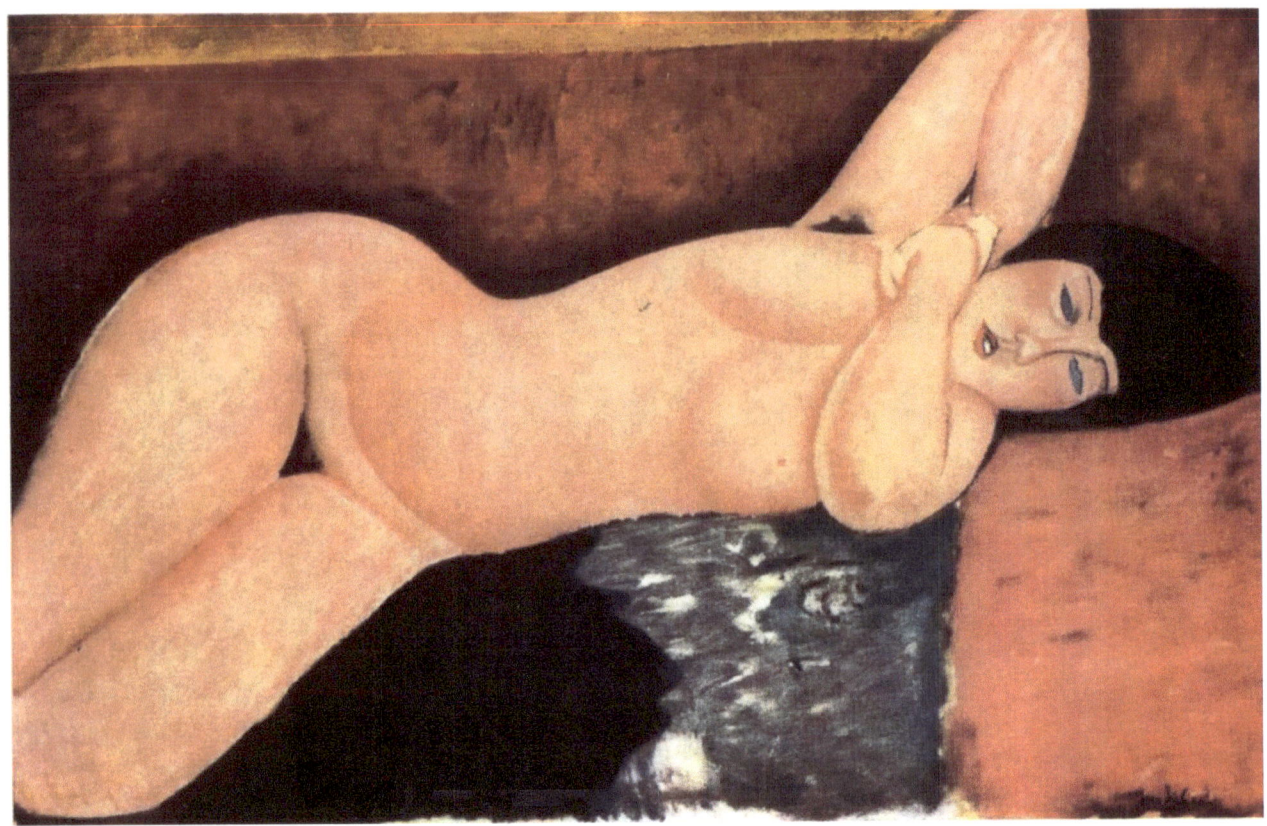

Reclining nude--1917

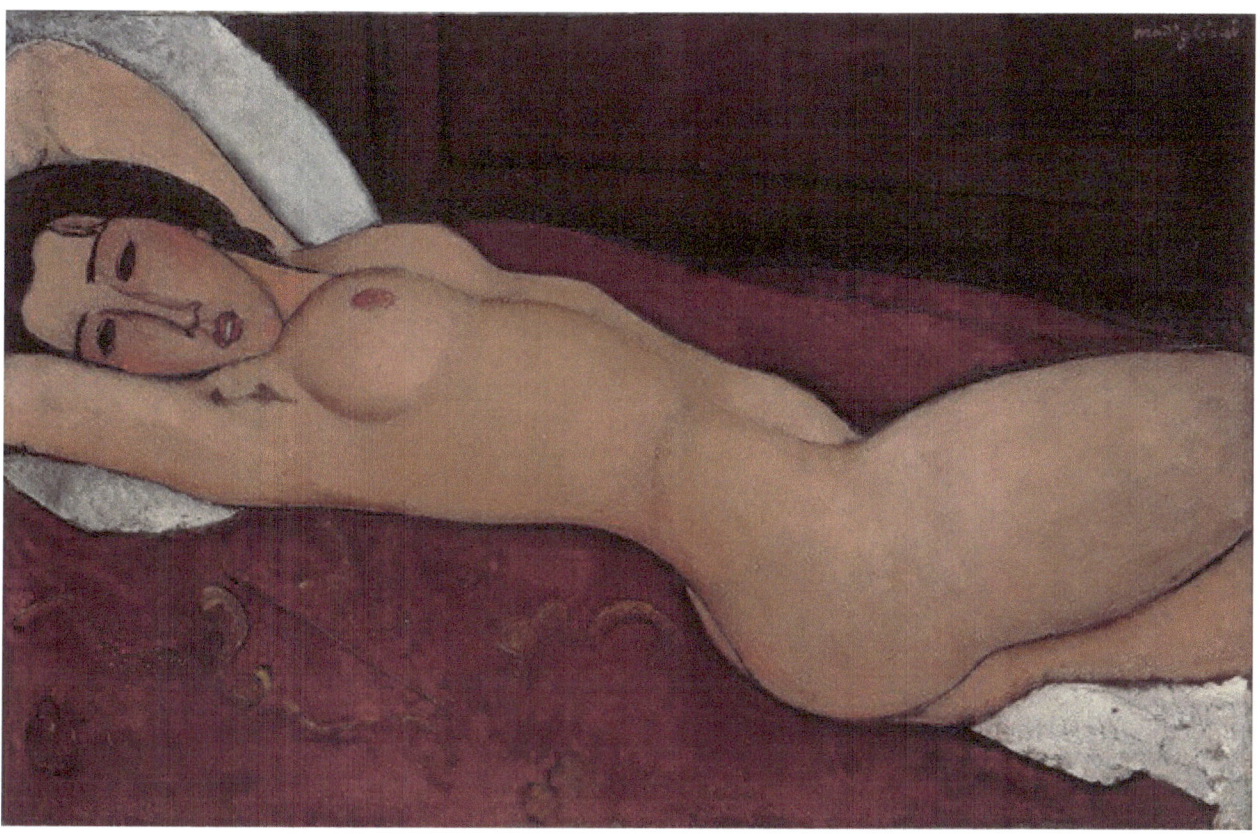

Reclining nude--1917

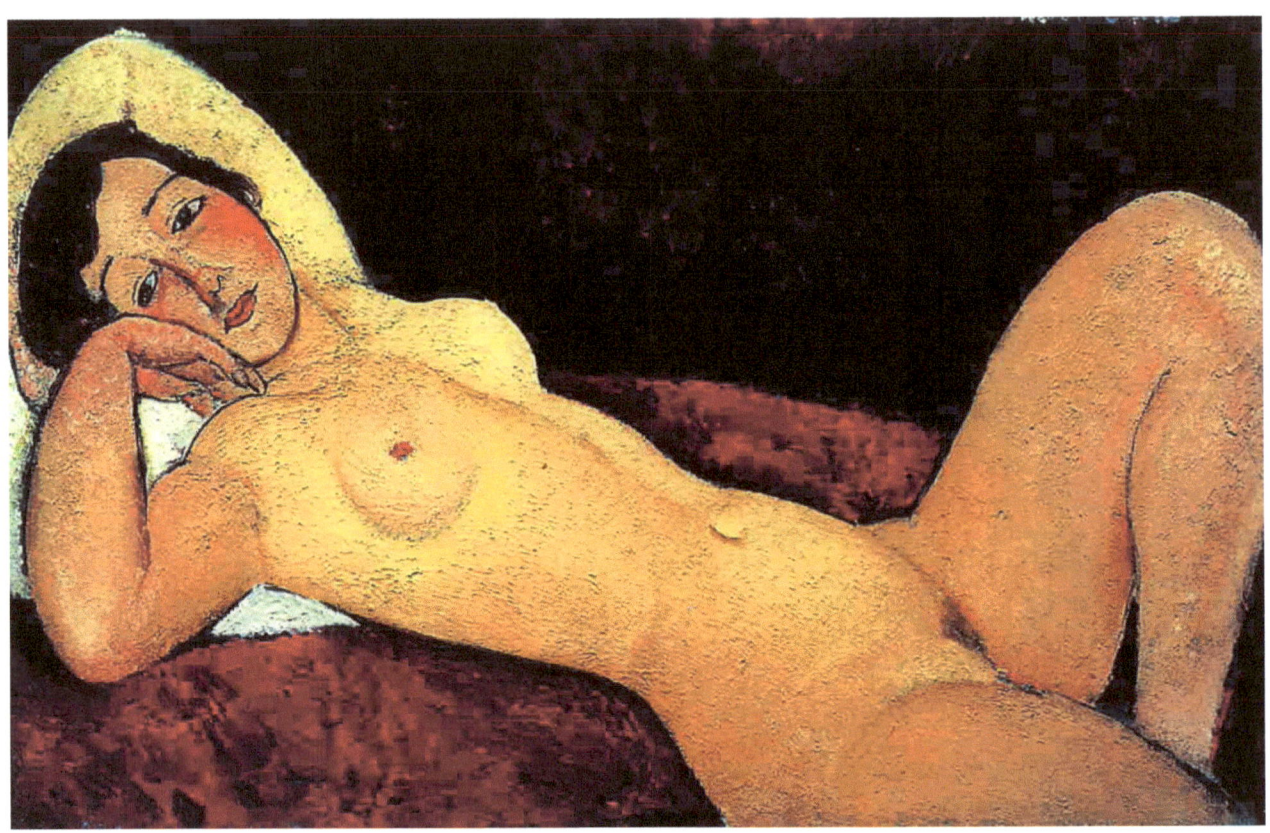

Reclining nude--1917

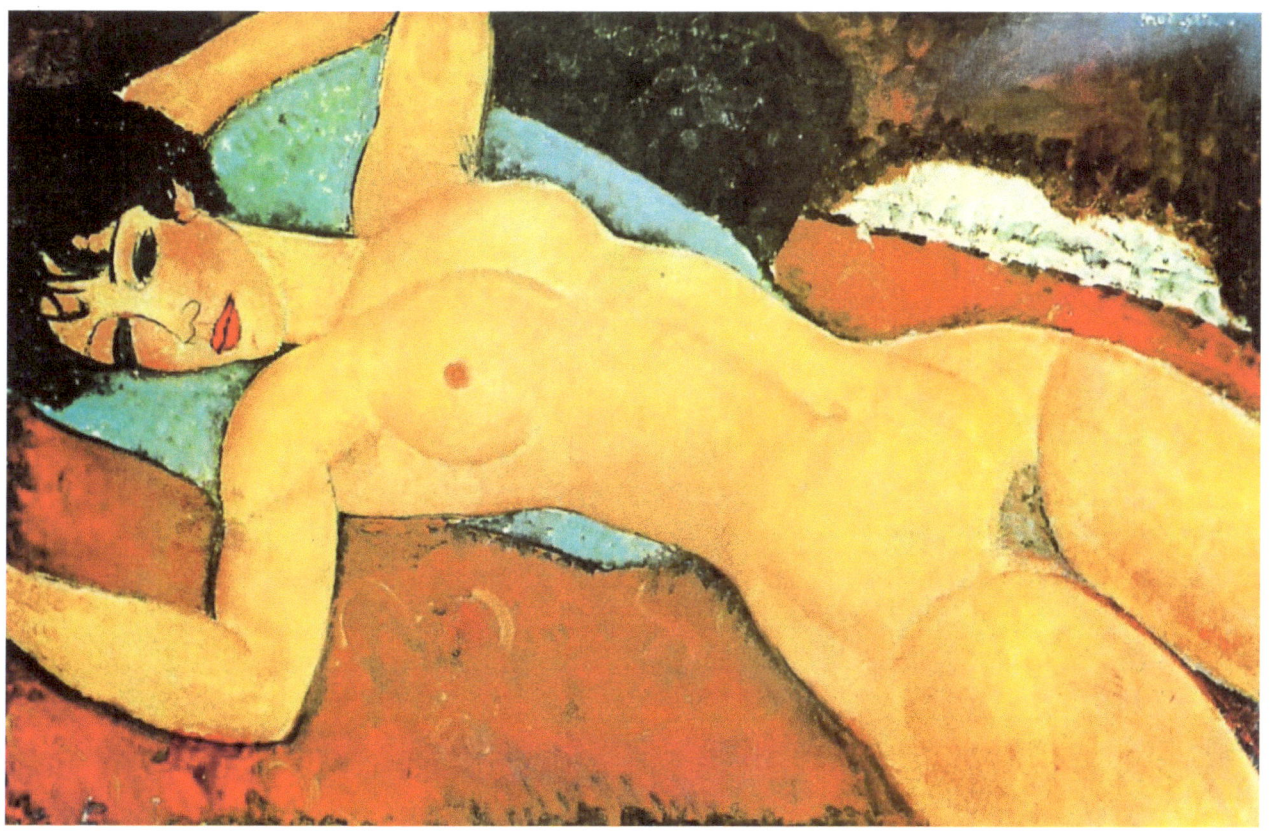

Sleeping Nude with Arms Open (Red Nude)--1917

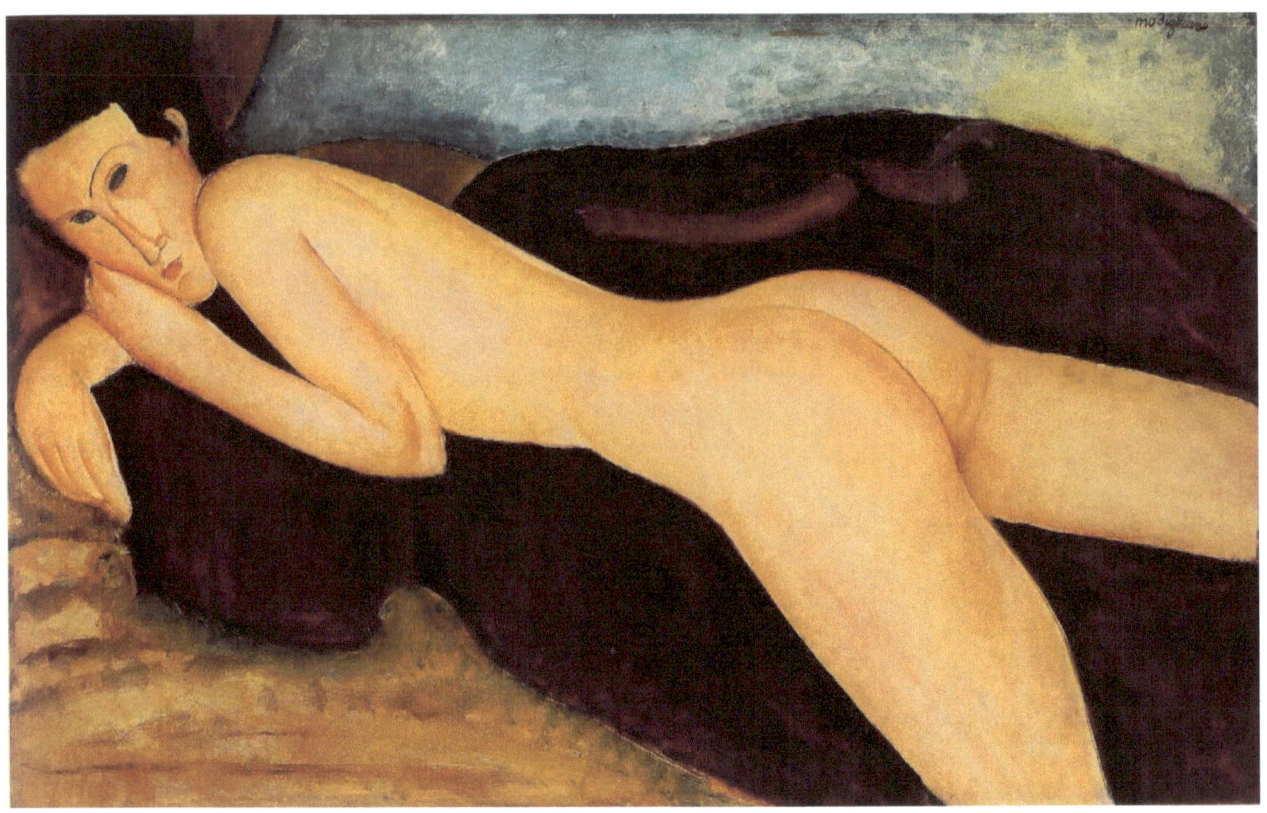

Reclining nude from the Back—1917

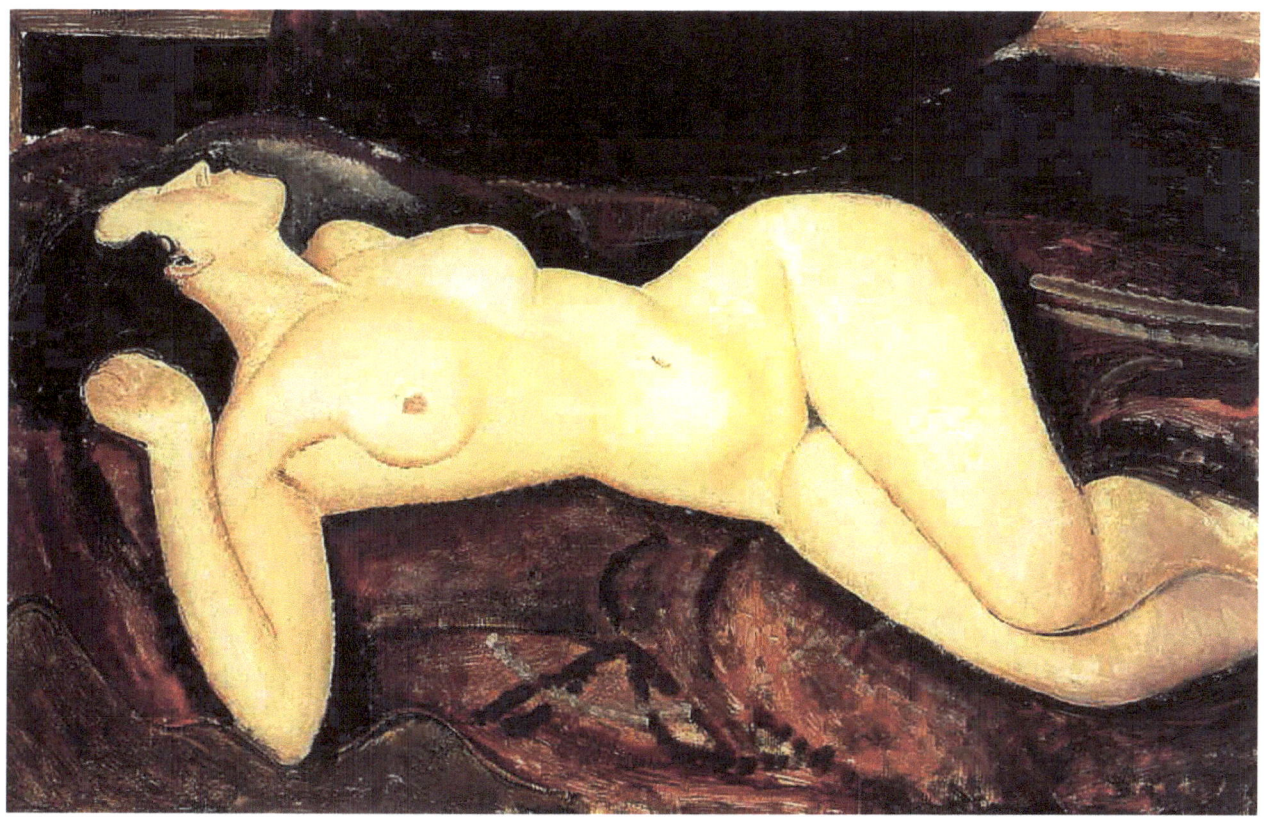

Recumbent nude--1917

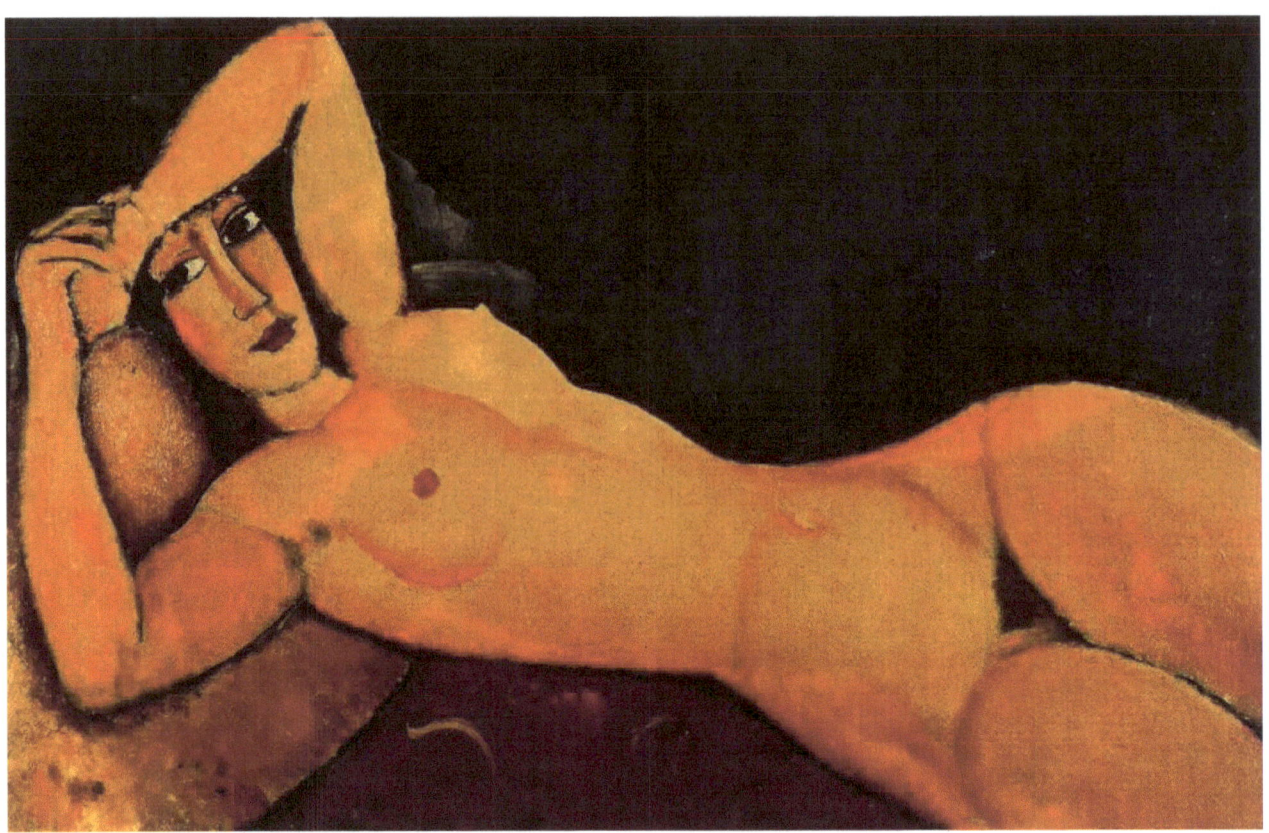

Reclining nude with Left Arm Resting on Forehead--1917

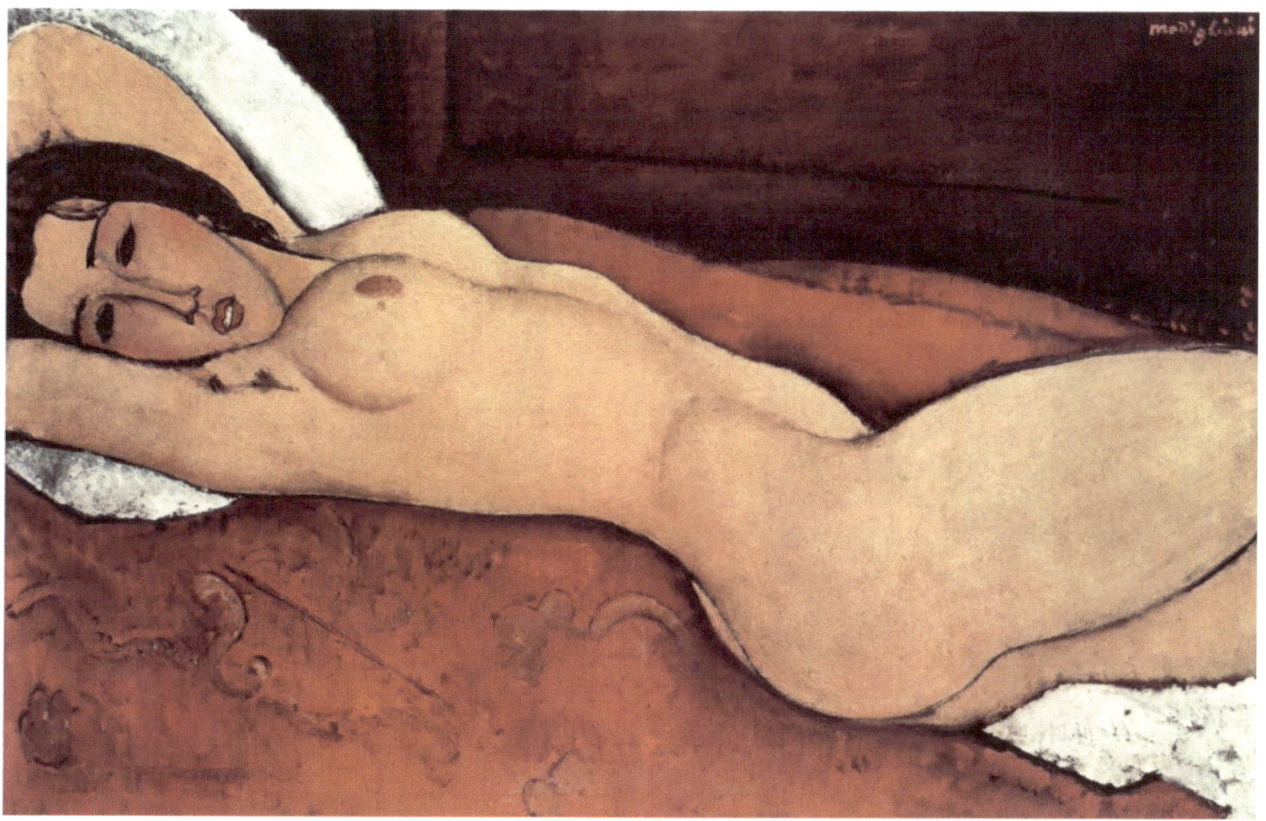

Reclining nude with folded arms behind her head—1917

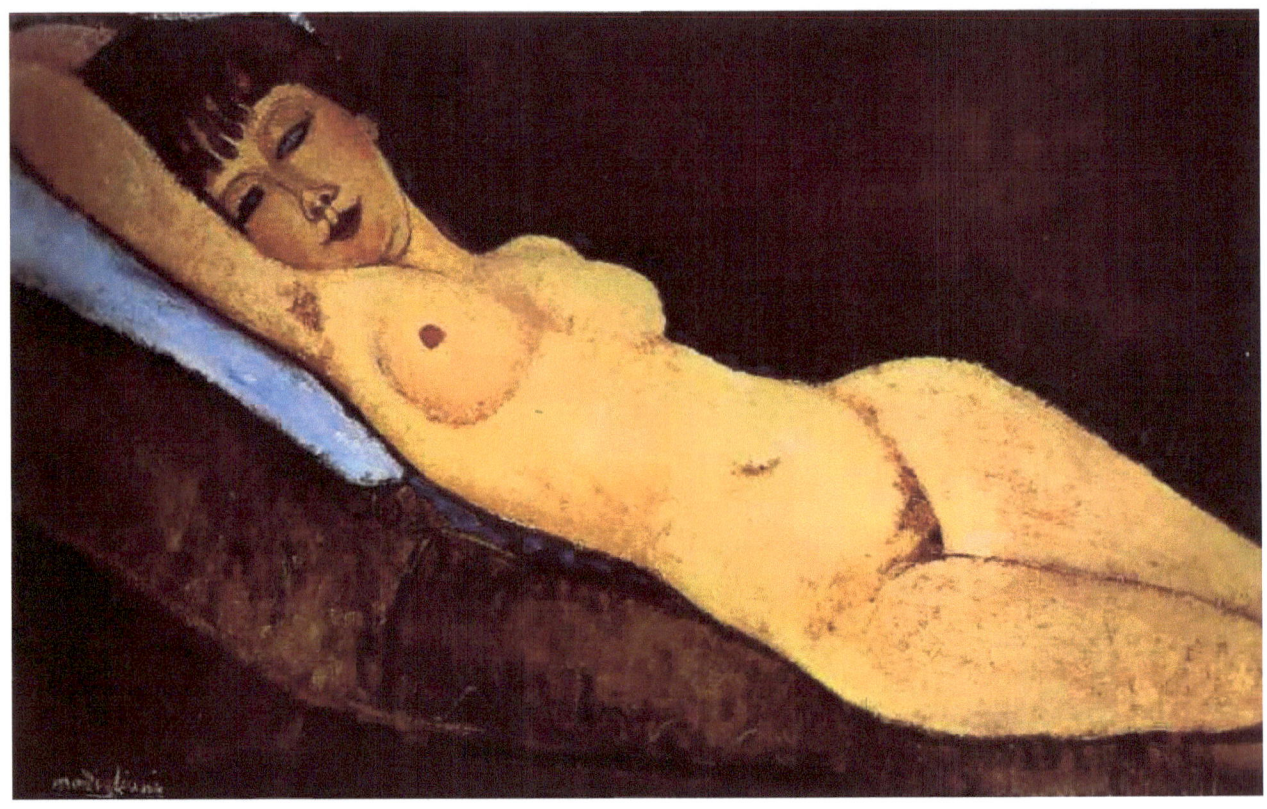

Reclining nude with Blue Cushion--1917

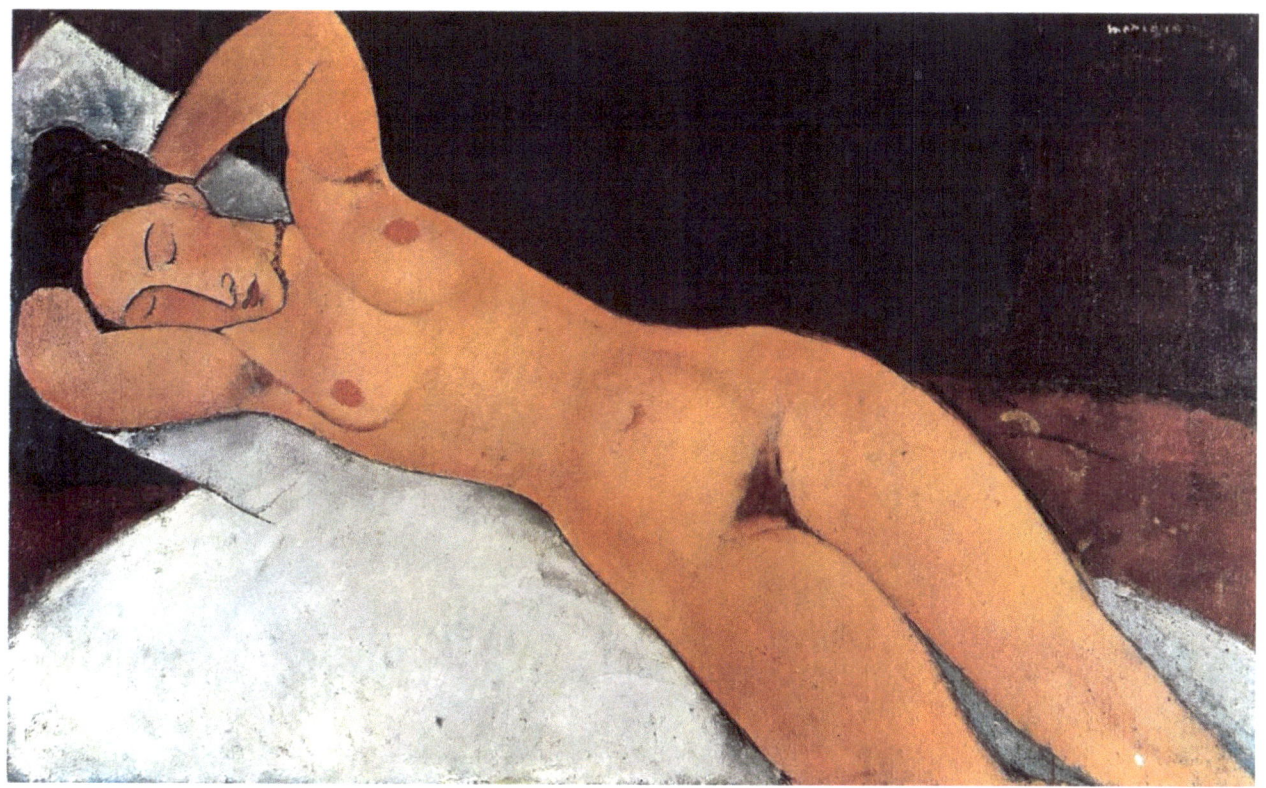

Nude—1917

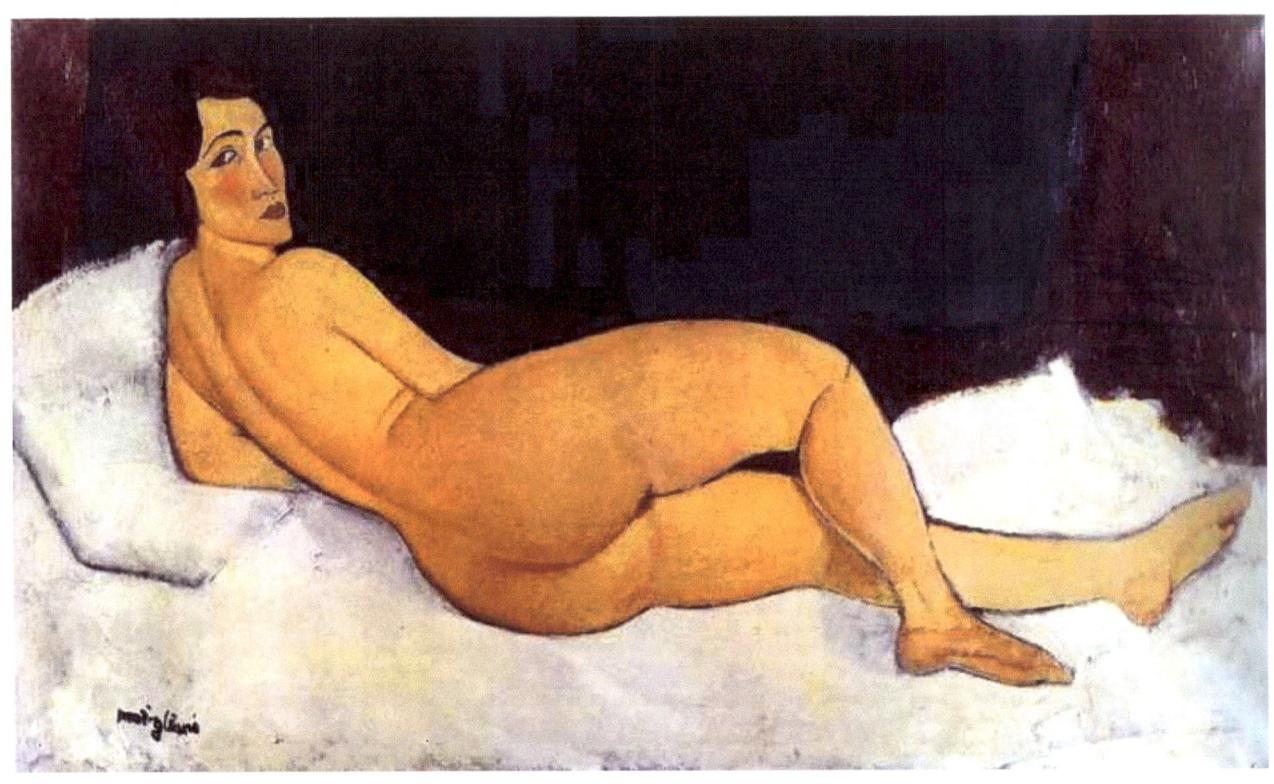

Nude Looking over Her Right Shoulder—1917

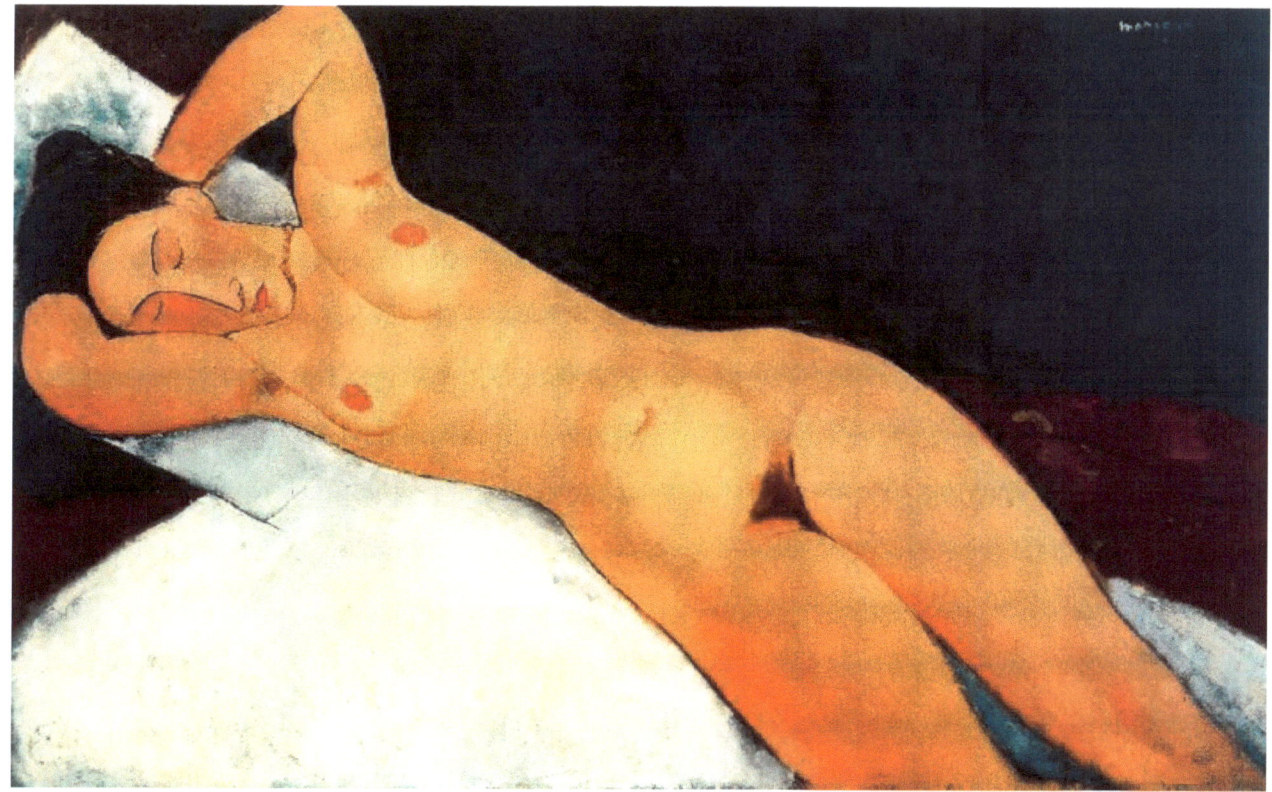

Nude with Necklace--1917

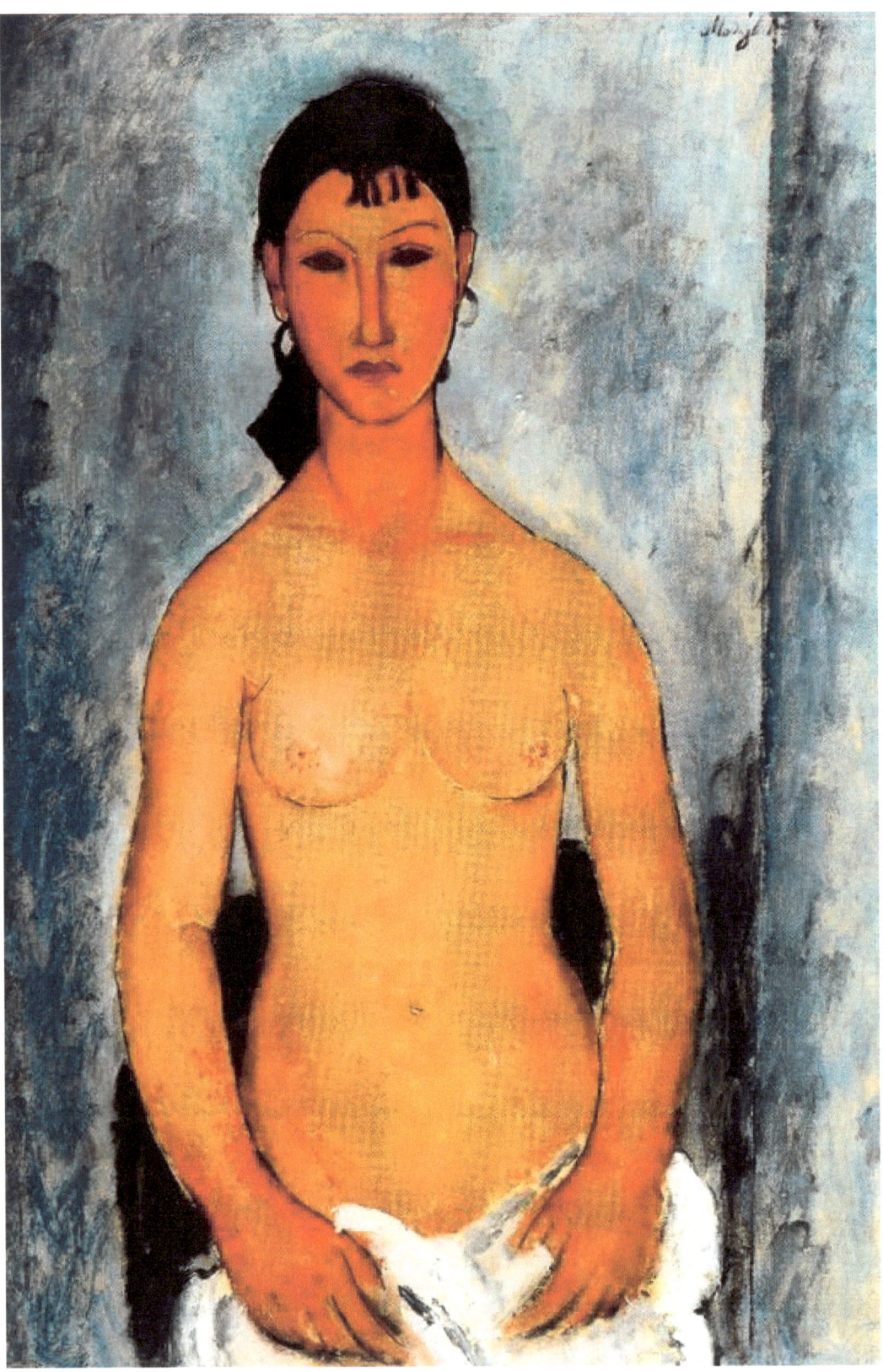

Standing nude (Elvira)--1918

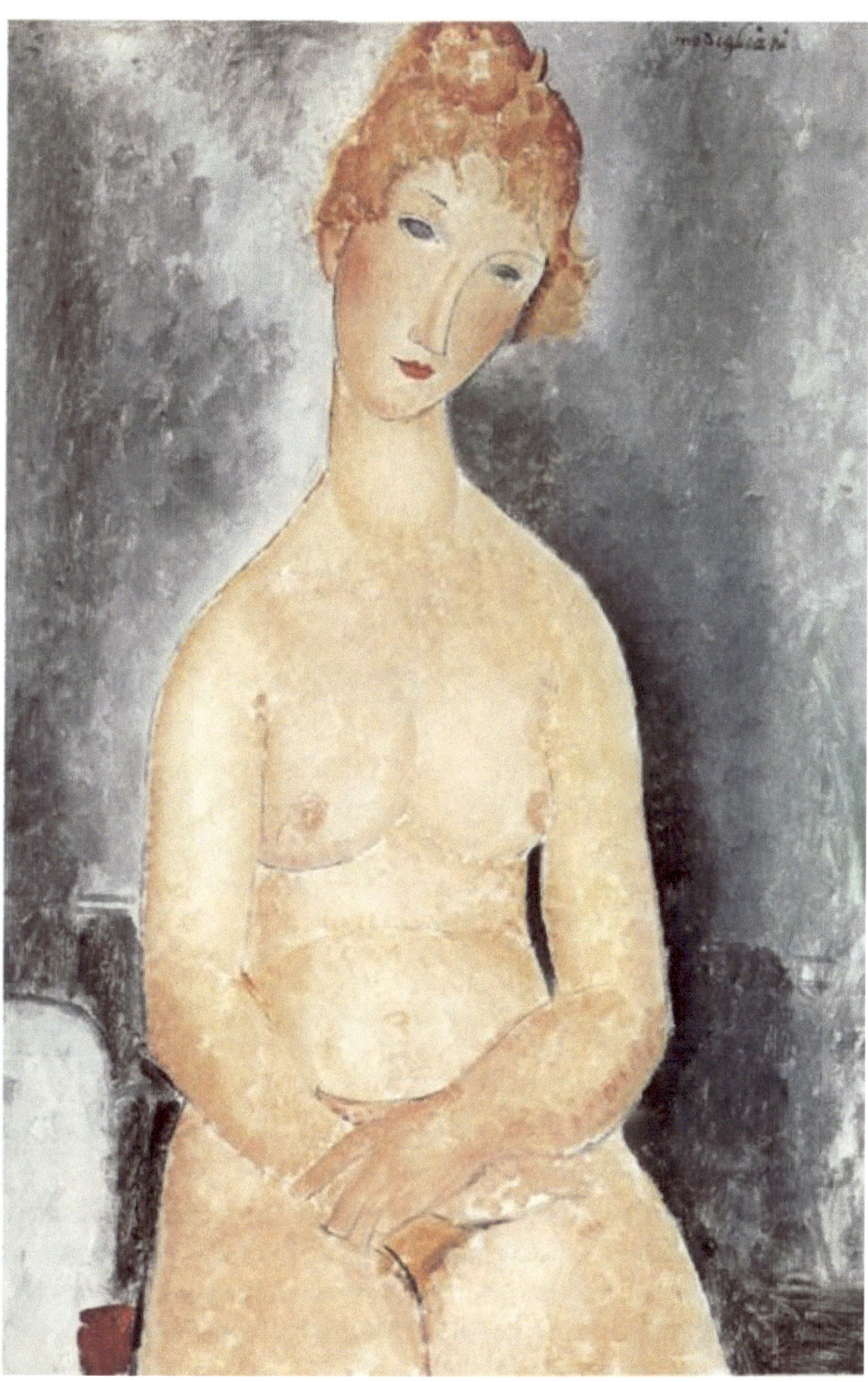

Seated nude--1918

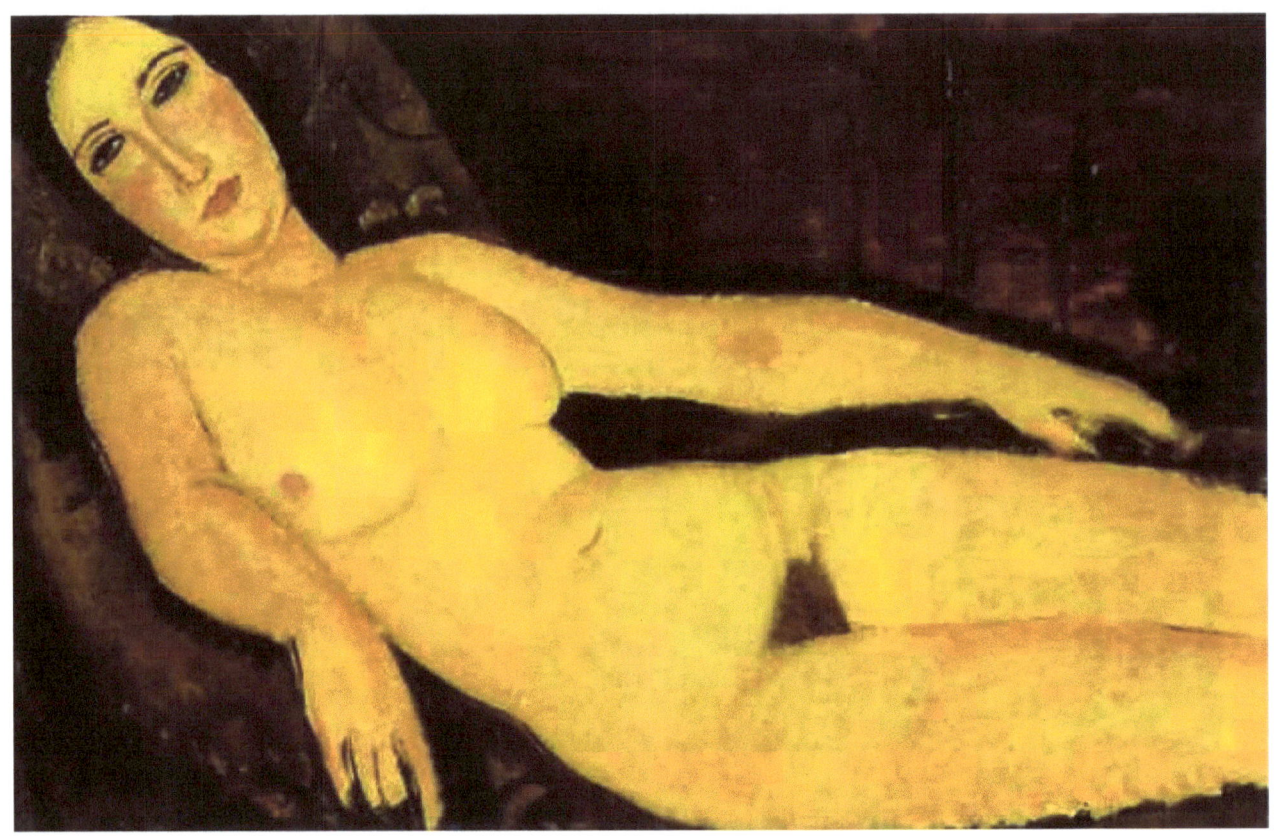

Nude on sofa—1918

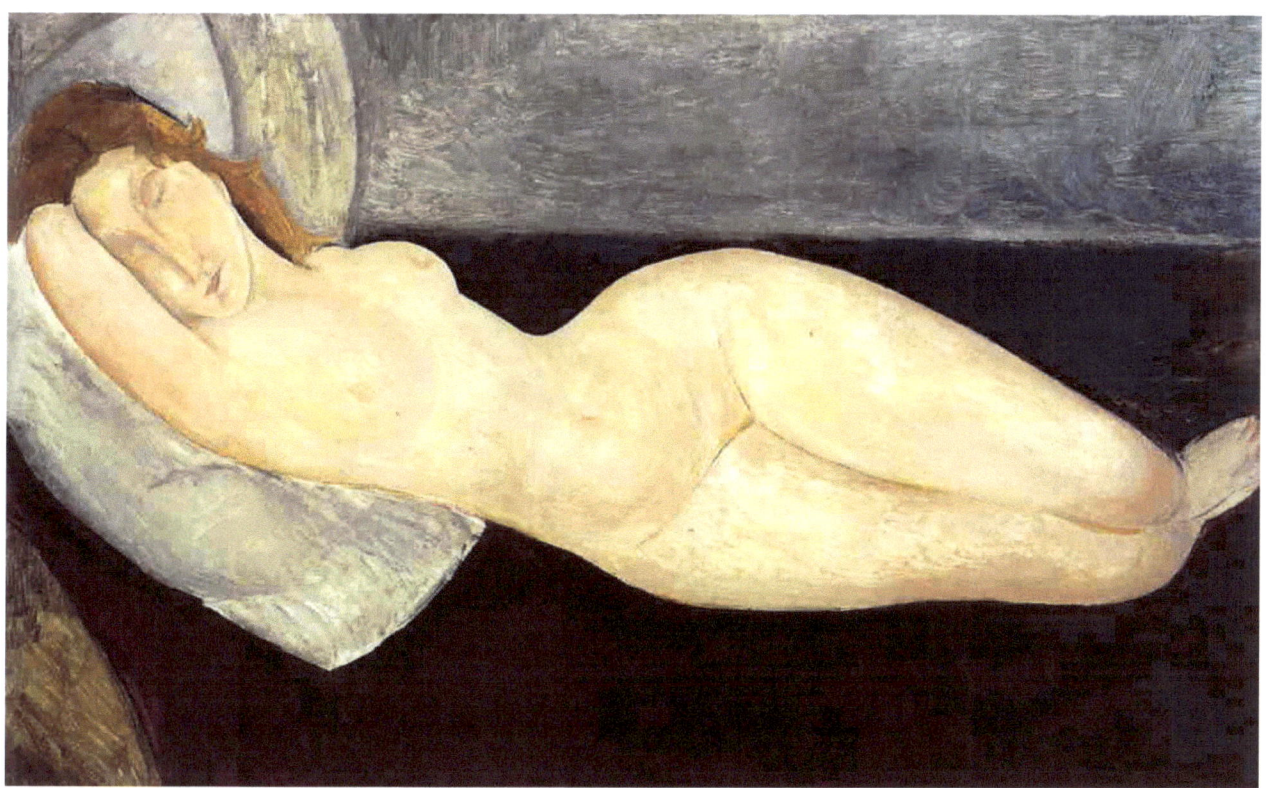

Reclining nude with head resting on right arm--1919

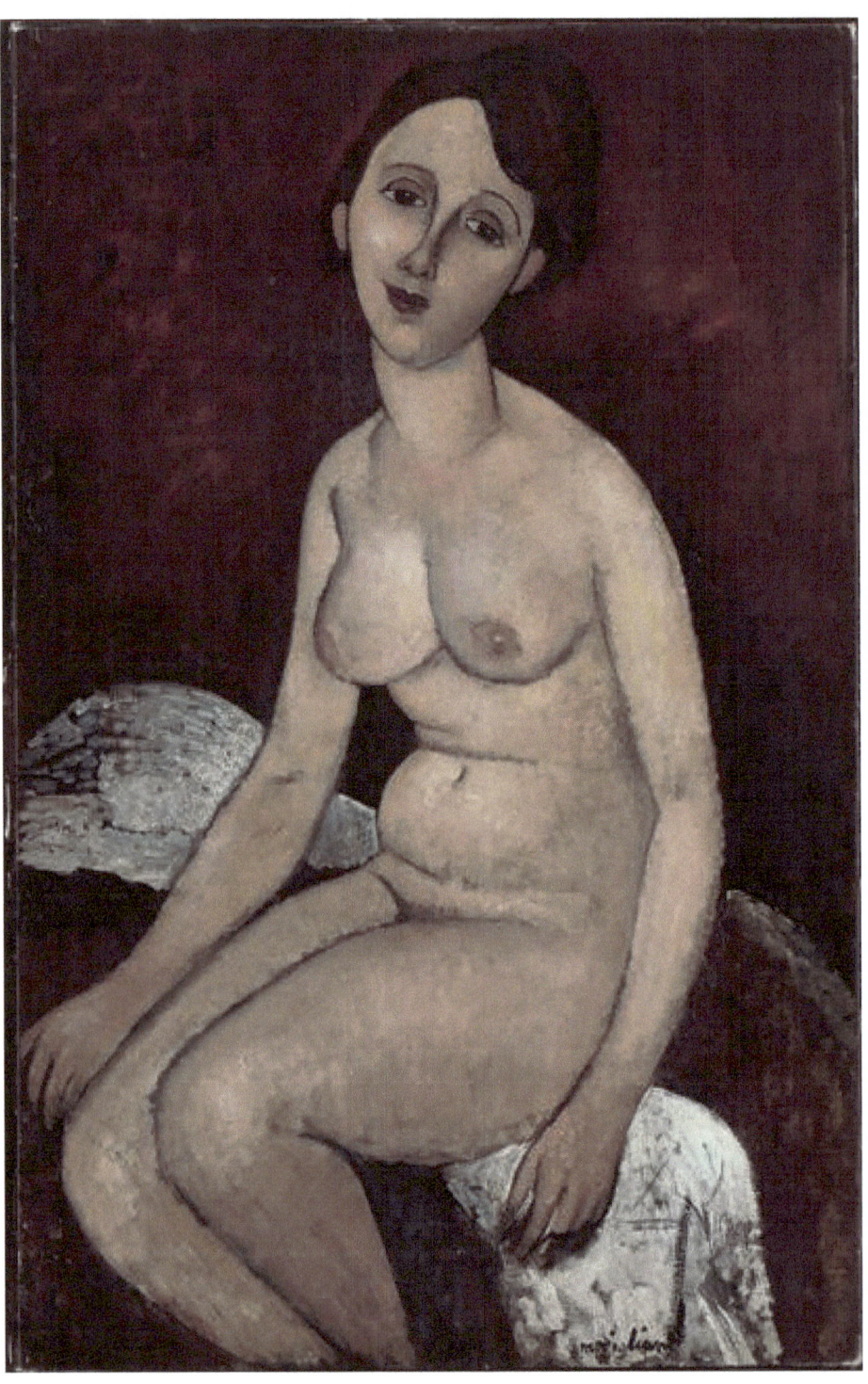

Seated nude

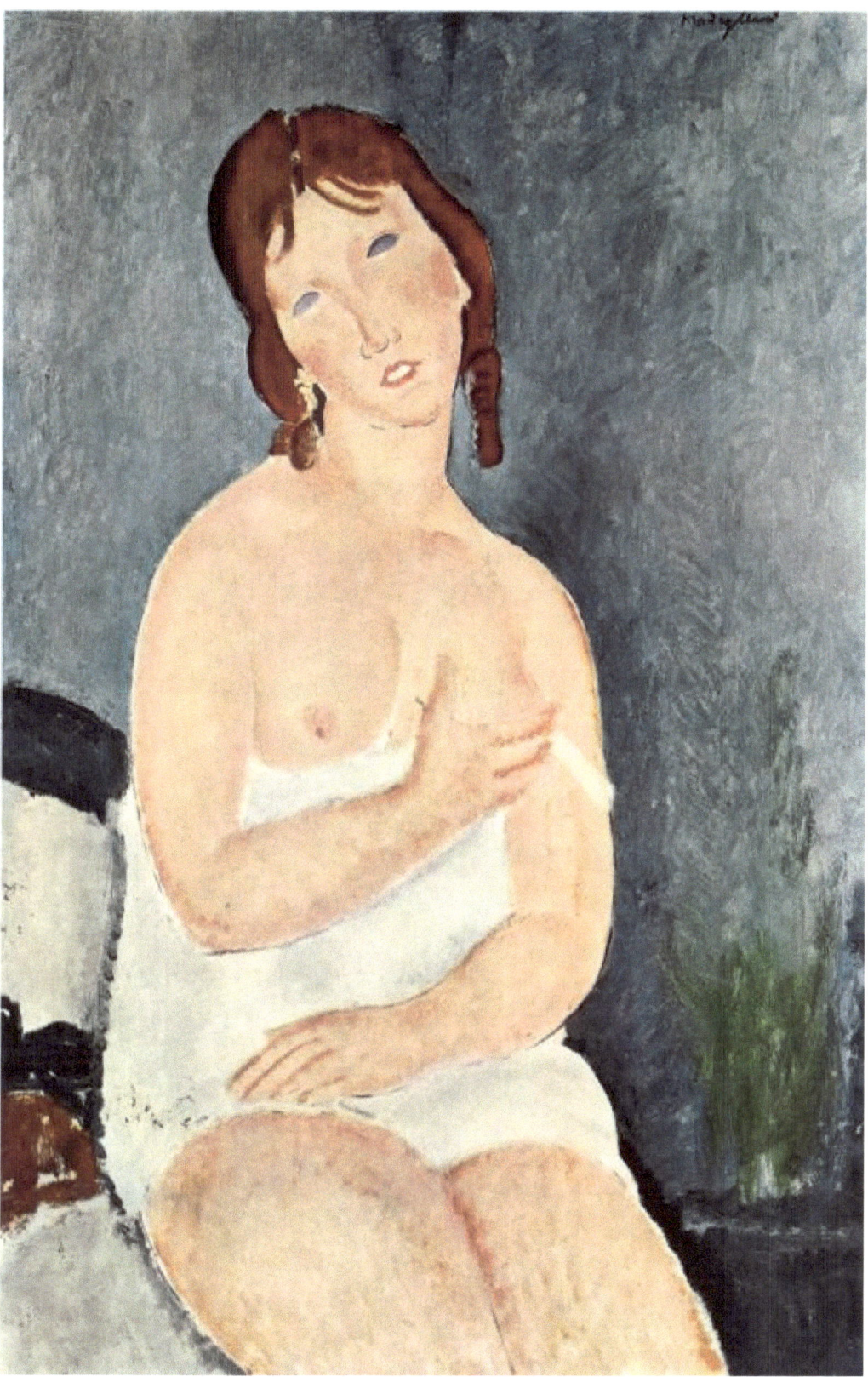

Young Woman in a Shirt (The Little Milkmaid)

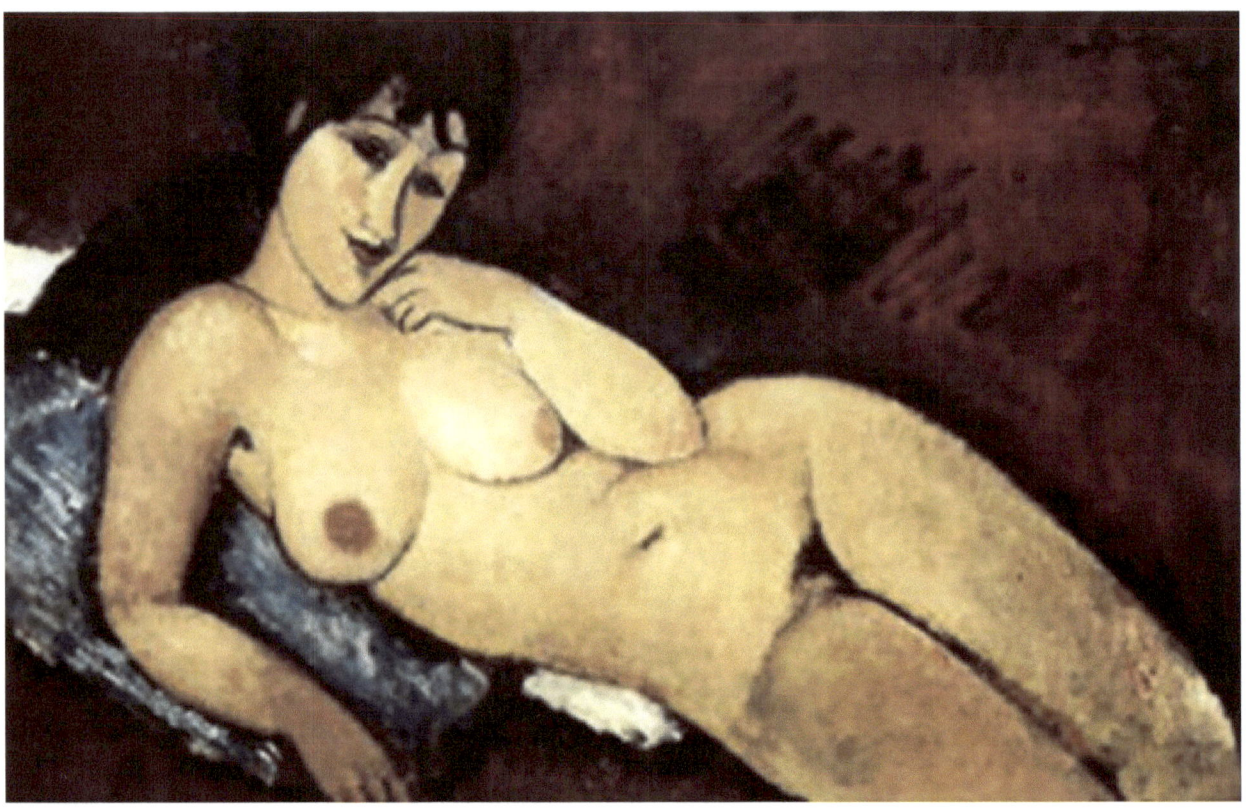

Nude on a Blue Cushion

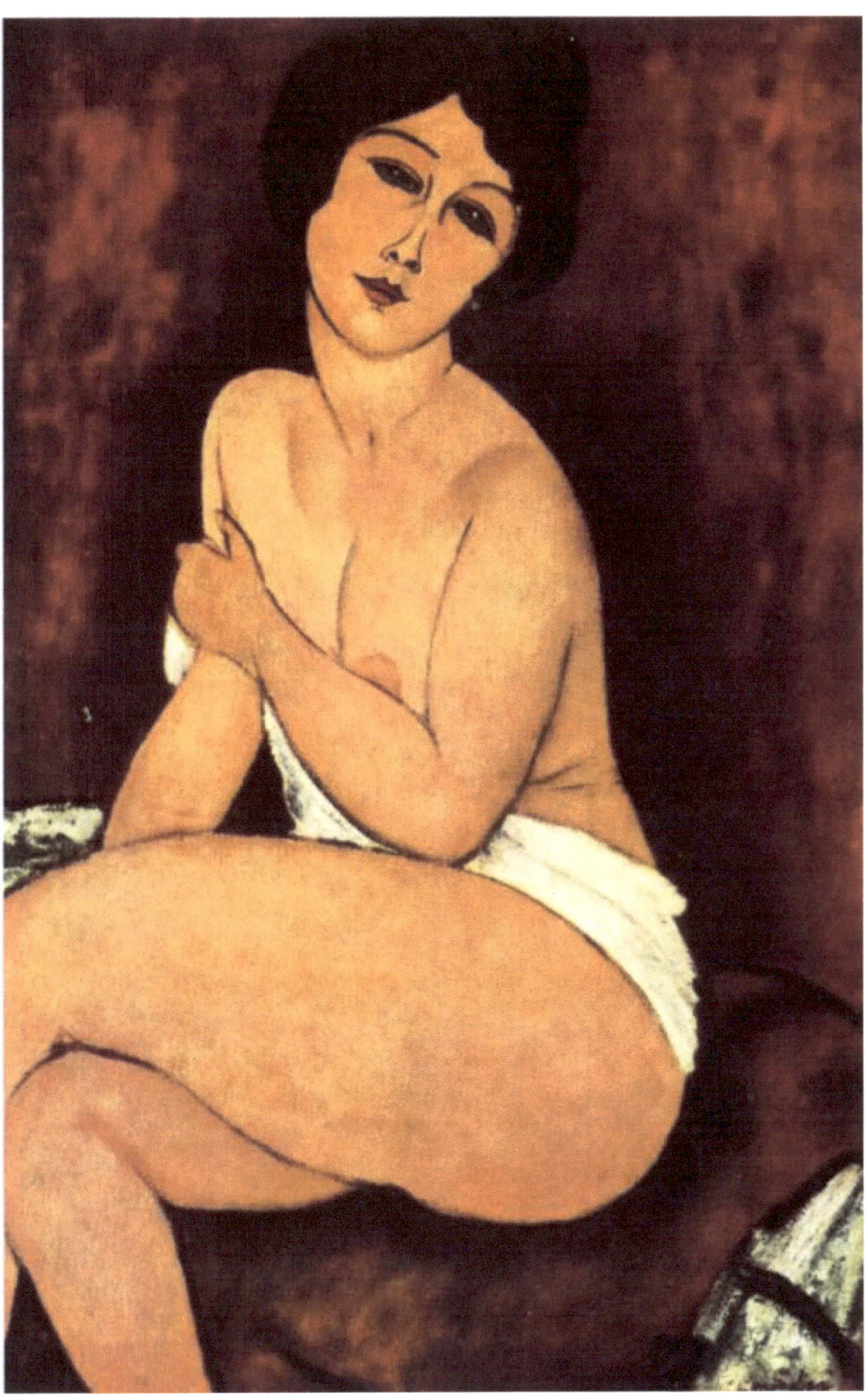

Large Seated nude

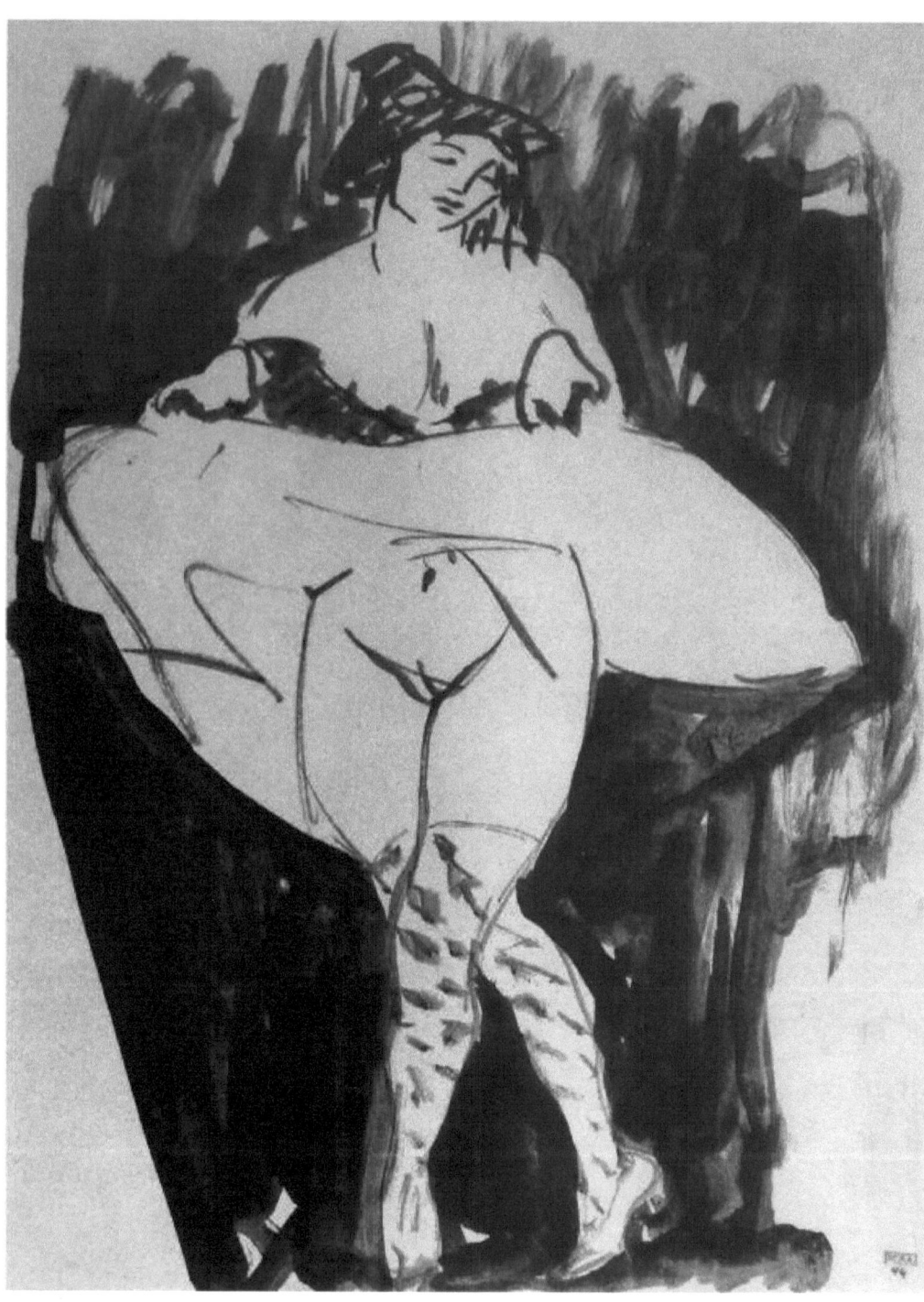

Dancer

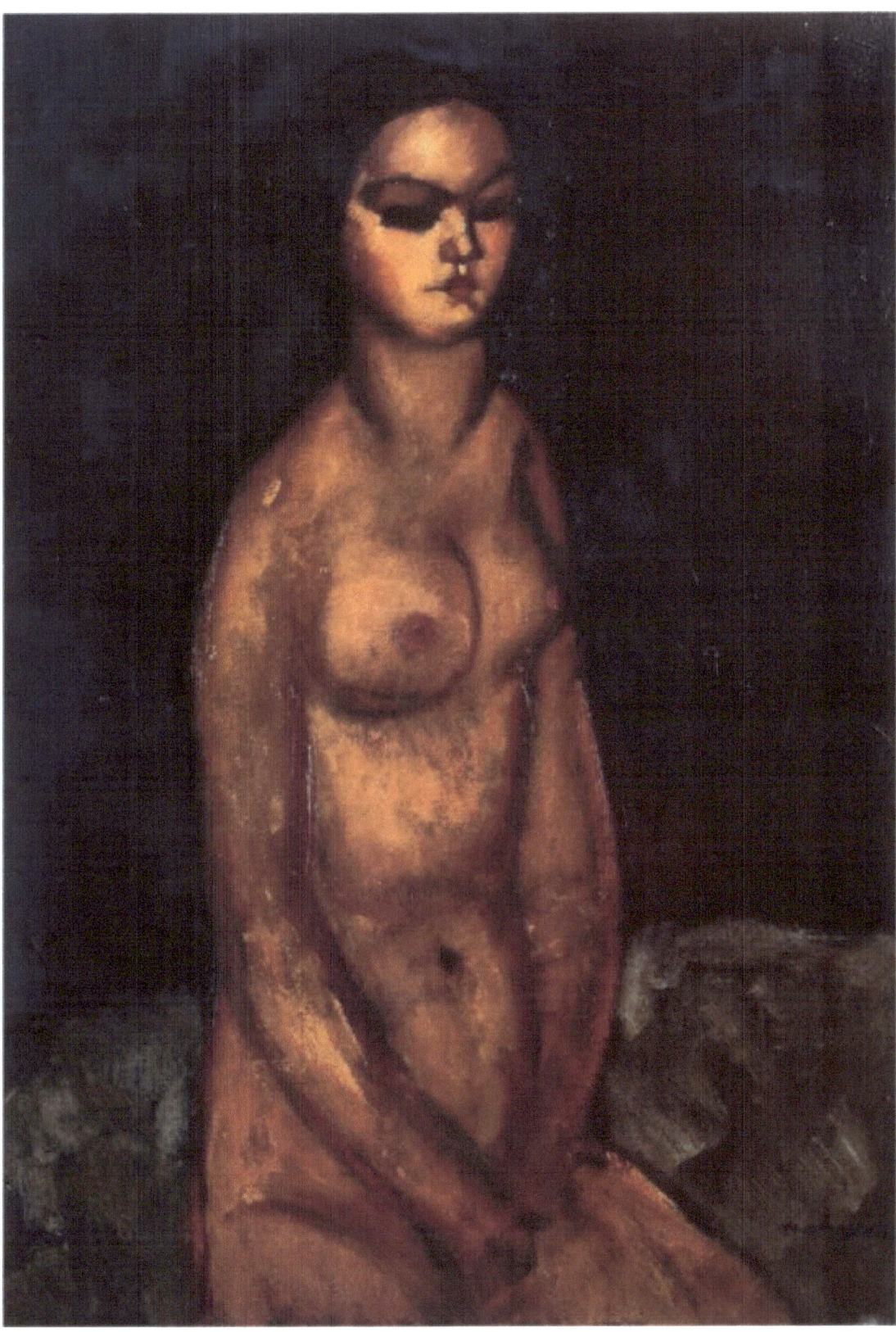

Seated nude--1908

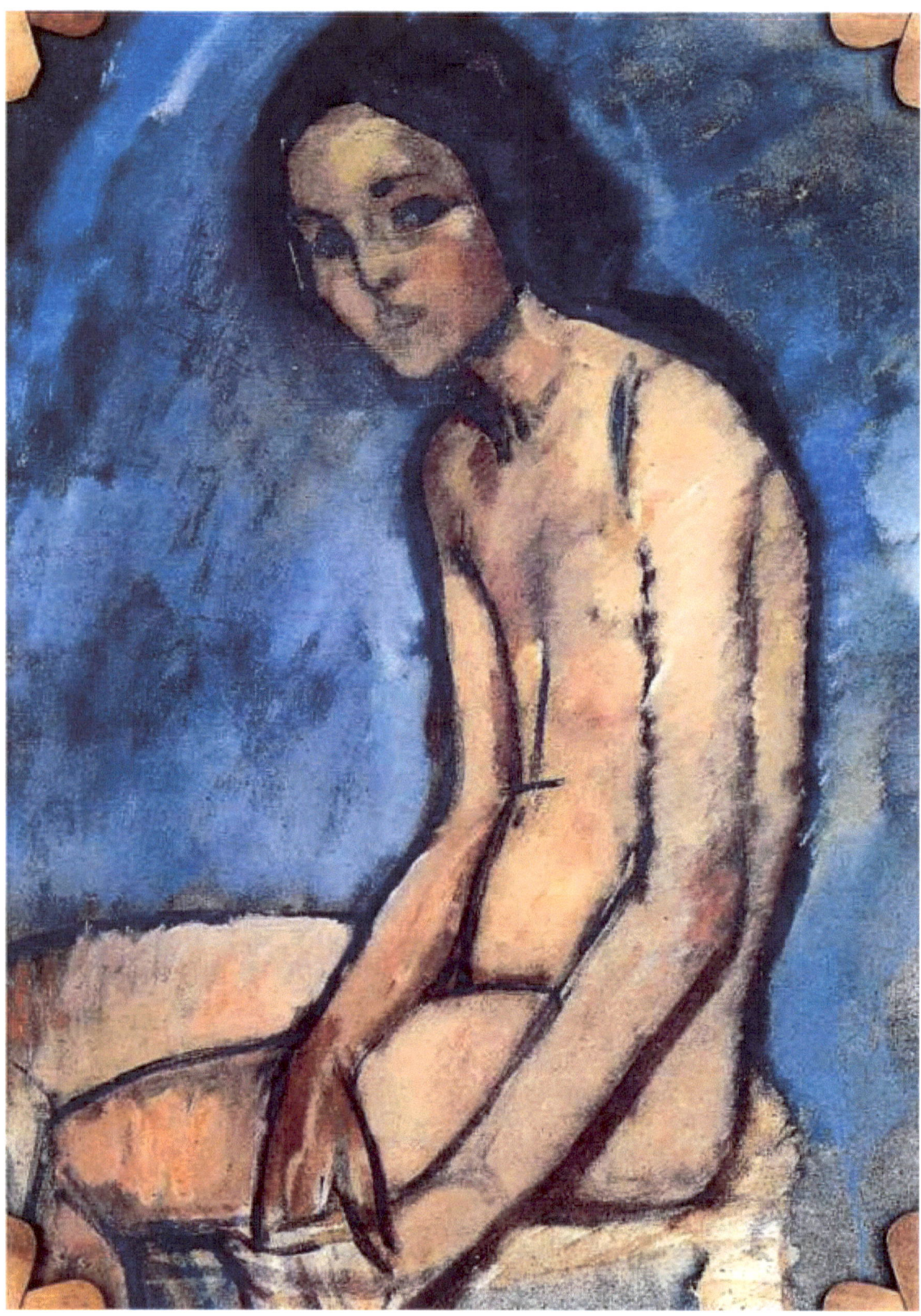

Seated nude--1909

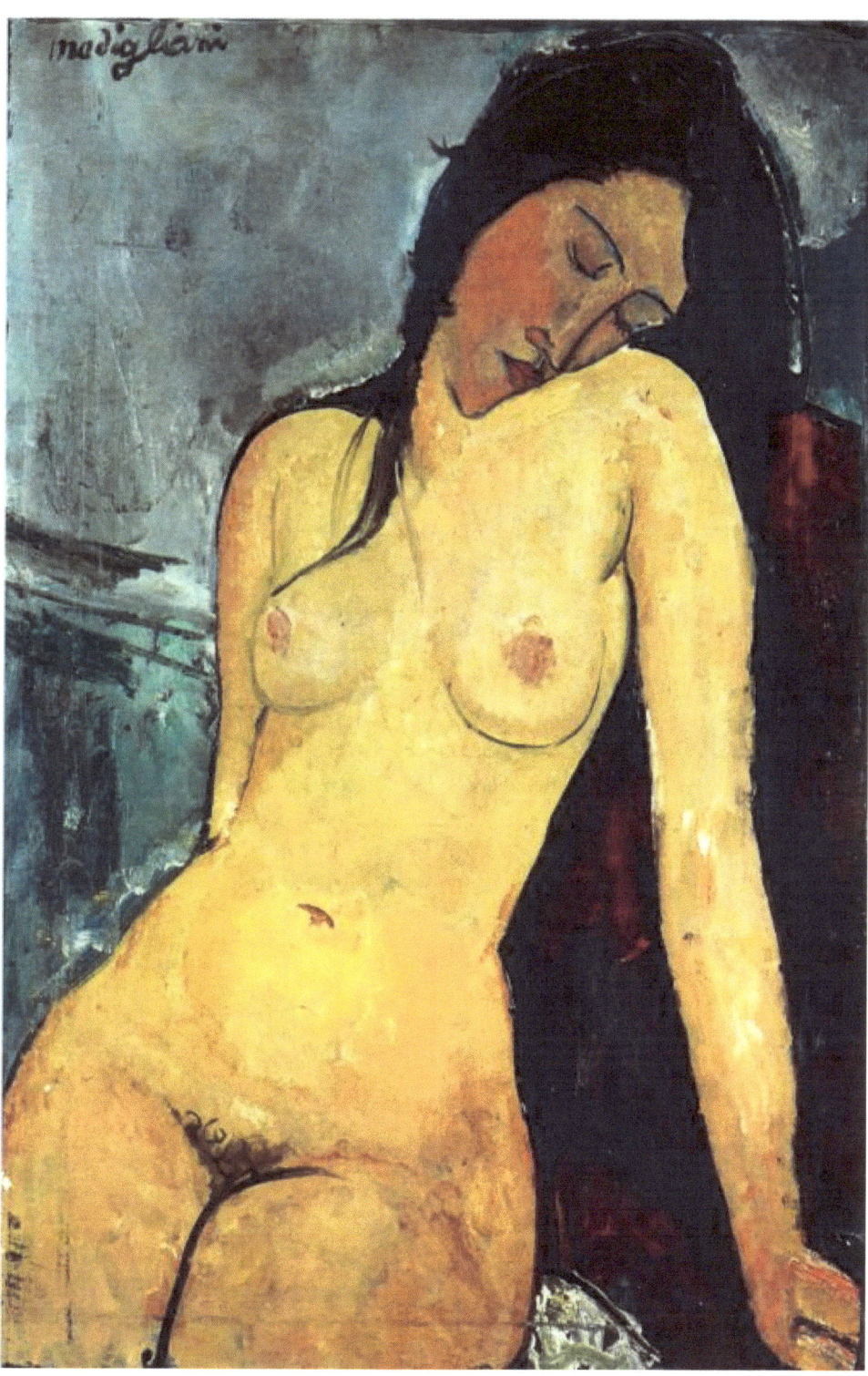

Seated female nude-- 1916

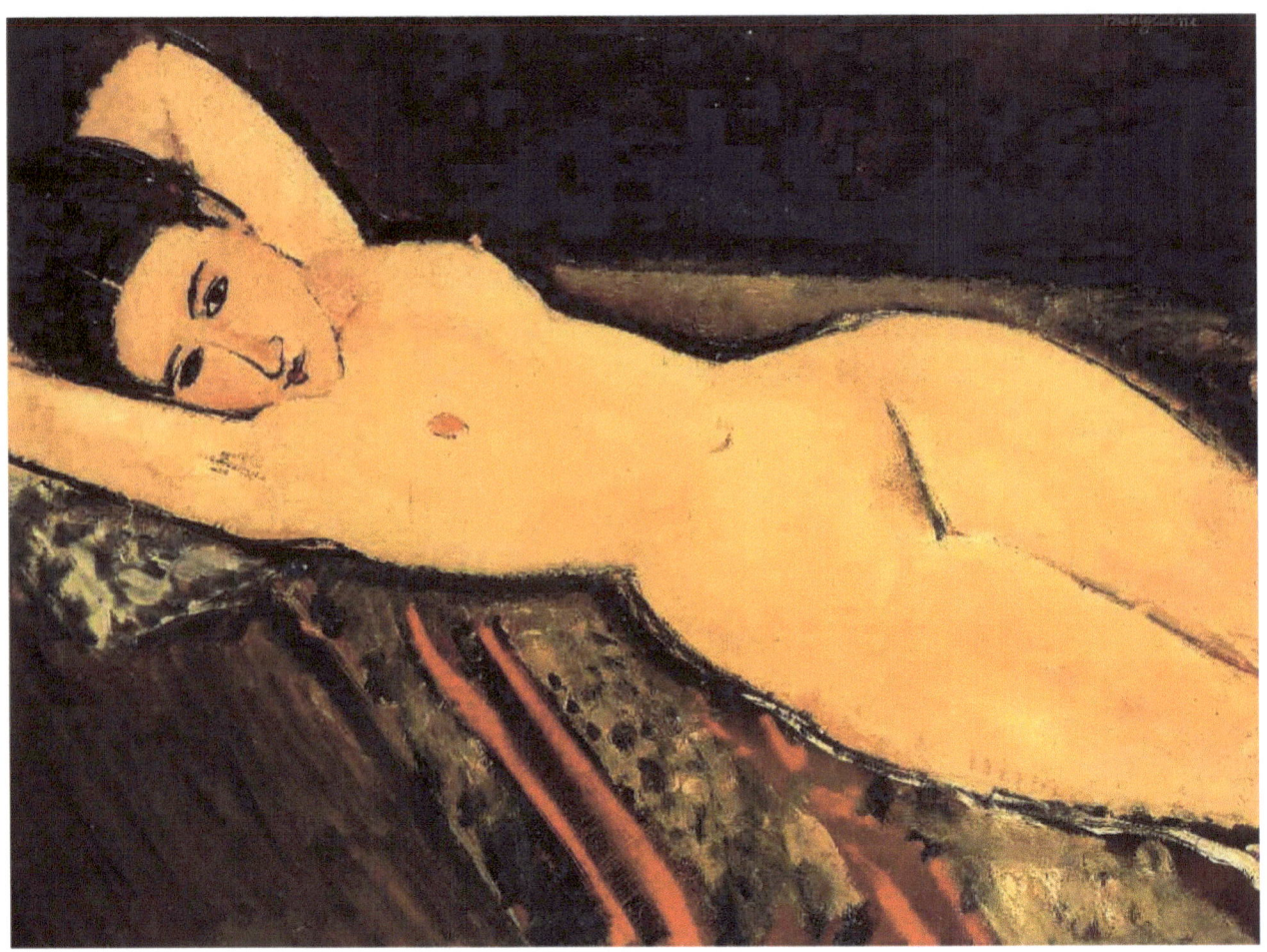

Reclining nude with Arms Folded under Her Head--1916